SMART GUIDE®

CREATIVE
HOMEOWNER®

vegetables

CREATIVE HOMEOWNER®, Upper Saddle River, New Jersey

First Published in North America in 2010 by
CREATIVE HOMEOWNER®, Upper Saddle River, NJ 07458

CRE︎ATIVE
HOMEOWNER®

TOUCAN BOOKS

TECHNICAL EDITOR	Liz Dobbs
DESIGNER	Phil Fitzgerald
EDITOR	Theresa Bebbington
PHOTO COORDINATOR	Christine Vincent
INDEXER	Michael Dent
PROOFREADER	Marion Dent
FRONT COVER PHOTOGRAPHY	Photoshot/Photos
	Horticultural/Andrea Jones

CREATIVE HOMEOWNER

VICE PRESIDENT AND PUBLISHER	Timothy O. Bakke
MANAGING EDITOR	Fran J. Donegan
ART DIRECTOR	David Geer
SENIOR EDITOR	Kathie Robitz
JUNIOR EDITOR	Angela Hanson
DIGITAL IMAGING SPECIALIST	Frank Dyer
PRODUCTION COORDINATOR	Sara M. Markowitz
SMART GUIDE® SERIES COVER DESIGN	Clarke Barre

Current Printing (last digit)
10 9 8 7 6 5 4 3 2 1

Manufactured in the United States of America

Smart Guide®: Vegetables, First Edition
Library of Congress Control Number: 2009932186
ISBN-10: 1-58011-476-8
ISBN-13: 978-1-58011-476-9

CREATIVE HOMEOWNER®
A Division of Federal Marketing Corp.
24 Park Way
Upper Saddle River, NJ 07458
www.creativehomeowner.com

Metric Conversion

Length

1 inch	25.4 mm
1 foot	0.3048 m
1 yard	0.9144 m
1 mile	1.61 km

Area

1 square inch	645 mm²
1 square foot	0.0929 m²
1 square yard	0.8361 m²
1 acre	4046.86 m²
1 square mile	2.59 km²

Volume

1 cubic inch	16.3870 cm³
1 cubic foot	0.03 m³
1 cubic yard	0.77 m³

Common Lumber Equivalents

Sizes: Metric cross sections are so close to their
U.S. sizes, as noted below, that for most purposes
they may be considered equivalents.

Dimensional lumber	1 x 2	19 x 38 mm
	1 x 4	19 x 89 mm
	2 x 2	38 x 38 mm
	2 x 4	38 x 89 mm
	2 x 6	38 x 140 mm
	2 x 8	38 x 184 mm
	2 x 10	38 x 235 mm
	2 x 12	38 x 286 mm
Sheet sizes	4 x 8 ft.	1200 x 2400 mm
	4 x 10 ft.	1200 x 3000 mm
Sheet thicknesses	¼ in.	6 mm
	⅜ in.	9 mm
	½ in.	12 mm
	¾ in.	19 mm
Stud/joist spacing	16 in. o.c.	400 mm o.c.
	24 in. o.c.	600 mm o.c.

Capacity

1 fluid ounce	29.57 mL
1 pint	473.18 mL
1 quart	1.14 L
1 gallon	3.79 L

Weight

1 ounce	28.35g
1 pound	0.45kg

Temperature

Celsius = Fahrenheit – 32 x ⅝
Fahrenheit = Celsius x 1.8 + 32

contents

part 1

creating a garden

The first decision you'll need to make is where to grow your vegetables. You might think the only place to grow them is in a dedicated vegetable plot. However, there are three easy ways to grow vegetables (and herbs and fruits) in any backyard, no matter how small: make space in your ornamental borders for vegetables that have decorative leaves, flowers, or fruit; build a raised bed or two—you'll be surprised how much a 4 × 10-foot (1.2 × 3m) bed can produce, especially if you refill it with a second round of vegetables as you harvest the first; and finally, grow vegetables in containers of potting mix placed near the kitchen door.

Explore your site and soil

If you choose to create a new vegetable plot, choose an open, sunny position that is sheltered from wind, and avoid areas where frost lingers the longest. Once you have a potential site in mind, it is time to investigate the soil in which your vegetables will flourish. One surefire way to improve any soil and produce better vegetables is to add well-rotted organic compost to the soil. It's also worth considering how you will reach your plot and move around within it—walkways that can be used year-round and are wide enough for you to move safely while carrying loads are ideal.

Plan your plantings

Buying seeds is the traditional approach to growing most vegetables, but these days there are other options. Buying young started plants that have already been germinated is worth considering. When growing in small areas, such as in gaps within borders, small raised beds, and containers, there is less waste if you choose started plants. But sowing seeds does score highly when plants, such as lettuce and other salad greens, are sown often throughout the growing season.

Care for your crops

The sowing and planting is not the end of your growing journey, but just the beginning. Your crops will need cultivating, and in the first few weeks while their roots are getting established you will need to make sure they have sufficient moisture, are not exposed to extreme weather, and are not crowded by weeds. Later, as the plants develop, you will have to make sure they are supplied with any extra nutrients they need and that pests and diseases don't get to your crops before you do.

Where Gardens Grow

You might think the only place to grow vegetables is in a dedicated kitchen garden, but no matter how small your backyard, there will be alternative opportunities: creating a raised bed filled with compost, incorporating vegetable plants among flower borders, and—last but not least—using containers.

How to Start

Most vegetable plants need sun and a moist but well-drained soil. If conditions are less than ideal, choose your plants carefully and be prepared to improve the soil and provide a bit more care. Of all the alternatives, the most useful is a raised-bed system.

Raised Beds

By marking out an area of ground that is not walked on and that is built up above the normal soil level by adding soil amendments or topsoil, you can create good growing conditions in a small area. Use several beds in a row or in a pattern with paths in between. There are a number of benefits to raising the soil level. Drainage is improved, and soil that was once cold and wet will warm up more quickly in spring, so you can start sowing vegetable seeds earlier.

A raised bed is home to an informal mix of leeks, lettuce, and flowers.

You can increase the depth of topsoil on poor thin soil. By keeping the walkways and growing areas separate, the soil in the beds won't become compacted underfoot, so there is no need to dig every year. The soil structure will remain more open, so roots will be able to get

Vegetables can be an attractive feature in any garden.

established faster. Compost, fertilizer, and water will be concentrated on the growing area, not the paths.

Raised-Bed Design

To gain the benefits of a standard raised bed, it needs to be only 6 inches (15cm) high, or 12 inches (30cm) if the soil is thin and poor. Ideally, the bed should be no more than 4 feet (1.2m) wide—any wider and you won't be able to reach the center without stepping into the bed. No longer than about 10 or 12 feet (3 or 3.6m) is best, otherwise you'll find it frustrating getting from one side to the other. Walkways between beds should be 12 inches (30cm) wide to allow for foot traffic; 18–24 inches (45–60cm) wide for a wheelbarrow. Mulching the paths with permeable plastic, gravel, or chipped bark will help to keep weeds down.

You can mark out a bed and paths by digging the bed and adding organic matter. However, enclosing a raised bed in a permanent edging, such as lumber, creates a neater finish, and you will be able to raise the bed surface even higher.

To create a high raised bed for gardeners who use a wheelchair or who don't want to bend or stoop, plan on a bed that is 24–30 inches (60–75cm) high for a wheelchair user or 3 feet (90cm) high for a standing gardener. Make it no more than 4 feet (1.2m) wide. To save topsoil, you can fill the bottom of the bed with building debris.

Making a Basic Raised Bed

To make a raised bed, start by marking out the area on the ground, making sure it is square. Cut 1×6s (2.5×15cm) into two 4-foot (1.2m) sections for the ends and two longer sections for the sides. Use galva-

Zucchini blossoms add color to a planting of lettuce.

nized screws or nails to attach them to 3×3 (7.5×7.5cm) posts 12 inches (30cm) long; these should be flush with the top of the boards—the rest will be buried to hold the bed in place. For long beds, nail a post to

Ornamental Vegetables

You can grow these colorful vegetables with ornamental plants in a flower border.

Annual Vegetables
- Bean, bush (yellow or purple podded types)
- Beet ('Bull's Blood' is colorful)
- Cabbage (red or savoy types)
- Carrot (ferny foliage)
- Chicory (especially radicchio)
- Eggplant (look for cultivars with purple foliage)
- Fennel (feathery foliage)
- Kale (especially Tuscan or red types)
- Kohlrabi (purple cultivars)
- Leek (blue-green foliage in winter)
- Lettuce (especially red and loose-leaf types)
- Okra (cultivars that produce purple pods)
- Asian greens (these are good winter fillers)
- Pepper (types that produce colorful peppers)
- Summer squash
- Swiss chard (types with colorful leaves or stems)
- Tomato (may need support)

Climbing Vegetables
- Bean, pole (with purple flowers or colorful beans)
- Cucumber
- Pea (tall cultivars tied to supports)
- Scarlet runner bean (cultivars with red flowers)
- Tomato (trained up a trellis)
- Winter squash (cultivars with small squash)

the center of each side, too. Dig a hole for each post. Level the top of the boards, excavating soil from beneath them if necessary. Pack soil into the holes until the boards are firmly in place. Dig the soil inside the bed as deeply as you can to loosen it, and add compost or well-rotted manure to fill the bed. You can dig this in or leave it as a mulch.

Beds and Borders

Many vegetables are also attractive annuals. (See "Ornamental Vegetables," left.) Use the less tender types, such as lettuce, to fill gaps or edge a bed early in spring; harvest them in early summer; and replace with annual flowers. As the year progresses, peppers, eggplant, tomatoes, and beans will add color. Make sure the vegetables have enough space, and be prepared to feed and water them. Winter-hardy plants, such as leeks, kale, and chicory, provide winter greenery. Perennial vegetables, such as globe artichoke, rhubarb, and asparagus, make attractive permanent additions to a large border. Climbing vegetables are good candidates for training on fences or freestanding tepees.

First, fork over the area; remove any weeds; and add some compost

and general-purpose plant food. Sow seeds in irregular patterns by making short rows or swirls; this will help you to tell the seedlings apart from any weeds. Plant transplants in groups or drifts as you would ornamentals. Water them well until they are established; then water with a liquid plant food every couple of weeks. Pests will still find vegetables in a flower border. Check regularly, and take action if necessary.

Leeks, on the right, blend seamlessly into this ornamental garden.

Vegetables in Containers

A bucket-size container with a 2-gallon (7.5L) capacity that is 12 inches (30cm) in diameter and depth filled with potting mix will suit most vegetables. Window boxes are ideal for herbs and salad greens, while hanging baskets suit herbs, small bush tomatoes, or strawberries. All containers need plenty of drainage holes; fill the bottom of larger tubs with gravel. You may have to water plants twice a day in summer, or install an automatic irrigation system. Plants will need feeding regularly through the growing season.

Where Gardens Grow

Soil

Before you start growing vegetables, you'll need to assess the soil in your plot. Some soil is naturally suited for growing vegetables, but most can benefit from the addition of compost and other amendments. By starting a compost pile, you will be able to recycle plant debris into free compost to help improve your soil.

Drainage

Vegetable plants prefer a soil that is free-draining. To check how well your soil drains, dig a hole 18 inches (45cm) deep in early spring. (Do not dig when the soil is frozen.) Fill the hole with water: if it drains away within an hour, you have free-draining soil; if it is still full the next day, it is extremely waterlogged.

Texture

Dig a couple of holes around the yard, and examine the soil that comes out. Soil that is wet and sticky or clings together in clumps has a high proportion of clay particles. If it separates easily into grains, it has a high proportion of sand. Look for a change of color—this can indicate that the soil is waterlogged in winter or there is a hard layer below the surface impeding drainage.

Clay can be hard to work into a fine soil for seeds, remains wet in winter, and is slow to warm up in the spring. It is fertile but benefits from plenty of bulky compost to open up

the soil texture. Sandy soil drains easily and warms up rapidly in the spring. It is easy to work but can be lacking in nutrients and can dry out in warm weather. Adding organic matter will increase its water-holding capacity and add nutrients.

Loamy soil with roughly equal proportions of sand and clay particles is ideal for growing vegetables.

Cultivating

Digging with a fork or spade will help break up compacted soil into smaller clumps. Do this in fall; leave the lumps over winter; and by spring the soil should have an open texture. Digging also allows organic matter to be incorporated deep into the soil and is an effective way to remove any perennial weed roots. If you have heavy soil, use a fork instead of a spade or shovel for digging. An alternative is to use a powered rotary tiller—and get the whole plot done at once.

If the soil has an open structure, you can simply add a thick layer of compost to the soil surface and leave it alone, rather than digging and turning the soil each fall or spring. The combination of plant roots and earthworms dragging the compost below

Add organic matter to the soil as you dig it to give your plants the best growing conditions.

the surface will improve the soil structure and add nutrients.

Organic Matter

Any soil will be improved by adding organic matter because it both opens up heavy clay and binds free-draining sandy soils. Other benefits include increased soil fertility and conserved moisture. Organic matter used as a generous surface mulch can prevent weed seeds in the soil

Sandy soil has large particles, which makes it free draining.

Loam soil has a crumbly texture and is made up of sand, clay, and silt.

Clay soil has tiny particles that trap water, leading to waterlogged soil.

Composting Ingredients

Below is a list of items you can add to your compost pile, and those you should avoid.

What to compost
- Lawn clippings (but not if treated with chemicals)
- Dead garden plants
- Remains of vegetable plants after harvest
- Shrub and hedge clippings (best shredded first)
- Vegetable trimmings, such as peels, from the kitchen
- Coffee grounds and other uncooked plant-based waste
- Cardboard (tear up or shred first, then add it in small quantities)
- Fallen leaves (if not using to make into leaf mold)
- Waste from certain pets, such as rabbits and guinea pigs (but not cats)
- Weeds (except mentioned below)

What not to compost
- Perennial weeds with their roots
- Annual weeds that have flowered or set seed
- Cooked food, bread, or meat, or food served with oil-based dressings
- Cat litter
- Garden plants with obvious pests or disease

Keep compost in a hidden area but near the house for convenience. A well-made compost pile will rot down into a soil-like material in under a year.

manure often contains bedding, too, and if this is mostly straw, it will break down into a good-quality compost. Avoid manure with a lot of sawdust because it takes a while to decompose. Well-rotted manure is best, but you can pile up fresh manure and cover it with a tarpaulin; after a year it should have decomposed enough to use in the garden. Poultry manure is too strong to use as a soil additive, but it makes a good organic fertilizer when well-rotted for several months. Soil improvers sold at garden centers may be based on peat, bark, or composted manure. These are convenient but expensive in the quantities needed to make a real difference to a vegetable garden.

Homemade Garden Compost
You can make your own compost with anything of plant origin from your garden or house. Build an enclosure out of old or recycled boards or rough-cut lumber. Make it at least a 3-foot (90cm) cube because this lets the material heat up during decomposition, which will help kill weed seeds and plant diseases. Use

four fence posts to form the corners, and nail boards to the sides and back. Nail two strips of wood inside the two front posts, creating grooves so you can slide loose boards down to make a removable front. A well-made compost pile will rot down into a soil-like material in six months to a year. Try to add material containing a mixture of one part moist green material to three parts dry woody material. To speed up the process, shred or chop the materials before adding them to the pile, and turn the pile to aerate it occasionally.

The composting material should be moist but not wet. Cover the pile to prevent rain from making it water-logged over winter, but water it, if necessary, in hot weather. If you are adding a lot of fresh green material, try including torn-up newspaper or cardboard to bulk it up. If you have enough material to fill them, build two enclosures side by side. Fill the extra one while the full enclosure is "maturing." When you empty the finished compost, refill it with half-composted material from the other. This mixing and aerating will kickstart the process all over again, and the pile will break down more quickly.

from germinating. There are different sources of organic matter, each with its own characteristics.

Although leaf mold adds bulk to the soil, it adds little in the way of nutrients. Rake up fallen leaves in the fall, and stack them in a pile or wire enclosure. After a year they should have broken down into a crumbly leaf mold. Animal manure has significant quantities of plant nutrients. Stable

Hardiness and Heat

For success in growing crops, it is important to choose the vegetables and their cultivars that will thrive in your climate. As well as knowing where to expect sunlight in your yard, you'll need to know how cold and hot it can get, and when to expect the first and last frost dates in your area. Your local Cooperative Extension Service can help you learn about your local climate, especially the frost dates, and these maps can be used as guidance, too.

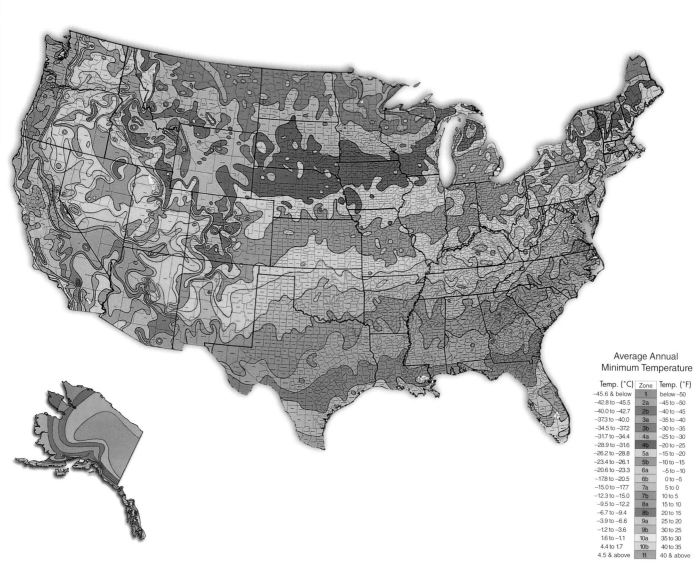

Average Annual Minimum Temperature

Temp. (°C)	Zone	Temp. (°F)
−45.6 & below	1	below −50
−42.8 to −45.5	2a	−45 to −50
−40.0 to −42.7	2b	−40 to −45
−37.3 to −40.0	3a	−35 to −40
−34.5 to −37.2	3b	−30 to −35
−31.7 to −34.4	4a	−25 to −30
−28.9 to −31.6	4b	−20 to −25
−26.2 to −28.8	5a	−15 to −20
−23.4 to −26.1	5b	−10 to −15
−20.6 to −23.3	6a	−5 to −10
−17.8 to −20.5	6b	0 to −5
−15.0 to −17.7	7a	5 to 0
−12.3 to −15.0	7b	10 to 5
−9.5 to −12.2	8a	15 to 10
−6.7 to −9.4	8b	20 to 15
−3.9 to −6.6	9a	25 to 20
−1.2 to −3.6	9b	30 to 25
1.6 to −1.1	10a	35 to 30
4.4 to 1.7	10b	40 to 35
4.5 & above	11	40 & above

United States Hardiness Zone Map

The United States Department of Agriculture (USDA) has developed a Hardiness Zone Map. In the map, various regions throughout the United States have been divided into zones based on records of the average minimum temperatures in those areas. Zone 1 has the coldest temperatures, while Zone 11 has the warmest. If you live in Hardy Zone 5, you can include plants that will thrive in Zones 1–4, too. When you buy seeds or transplants, the labels often include the hardy zones in which the plants will survive. Within these zones, there are smaller microclimates, so you should use this information only as a guide and try experimenting.

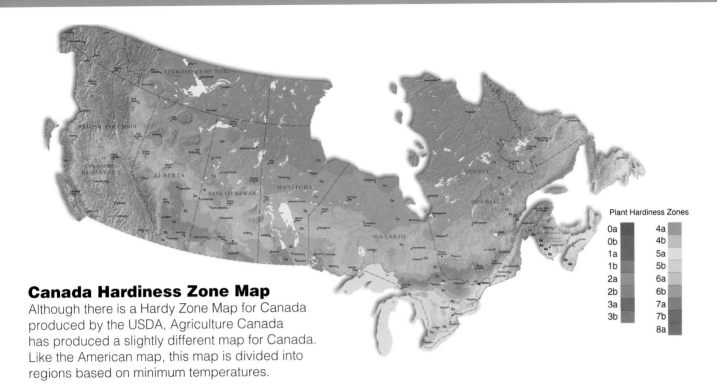

Canada Hardiness Zone Map

Although there is a Hardy Zone Map for Canada produced by the USDA, Agriculture Canada has produced a slightly different map for Canada. Like the American map, this map is divided into regions based on minimum temperatures.

Plant Hardiness Zones

0a	4a
0b	4b
1a	5a
1b	5b
2a	6a
2b	6b
3a	7a
3b	7b
	8a

Hardiness and Heat

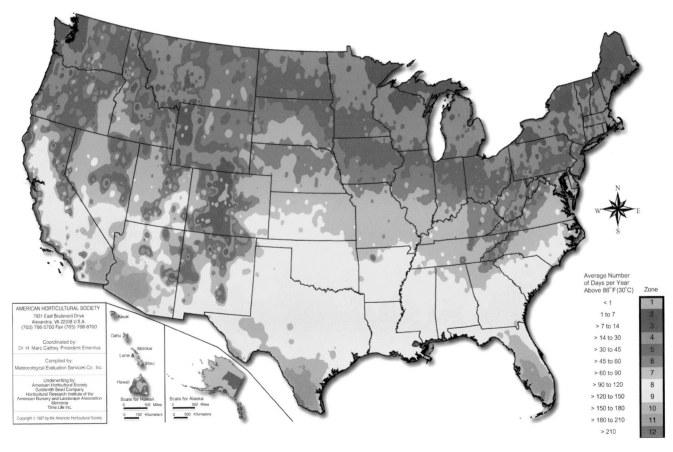

AMERICAN HORTICULTURAL SOCIETY
7931 East Boulevard Drive
Alexandria, VA 22308 U.S.A.
(703) 768-5700 Fax (703) 768-8700

Coordinated by:
Dr. H. Marc Cathey, President Emeritus

Compiled by:
Meteorological Evaluation Services Co., Inc.

Underwriting by:
American Horticultural Society
Goldsmith Seed Company
Horticultural Research Institute of the
American Nursery and Landscape Association
Monrovia
Time Life Inc.

Copyright © 1997 by the American Horticultural Society

Scale for Hawaii
0   100 Miles
0   100 Kilometers

Scale for Alaska
0   500 Miles
0   500 Kilometers

Average Number of Days per Year Above 86°F (30°C)	Zone
< 1	1
1 to 7	2
> 7 to 14	3
> 14 to 30	4
> 30 to 45	5
> 45 to 60	6
> 60 to 90	7
> 90 to 120	8
> 120 to 150	9
> 150 to 180	10
> 180 to 210	11
> 210	12

United States Heat Zone Map

The American Horticultural Society (AHS) introduced their Heat Zone Map in 1998. It divides the United States into 12 zones, each one based on the average number of days over 86°F (30°C) for the region—these are known as "heat days." If you live in Zone 1, don't expect any days above 86°F (30°C), while Zone 12 will have 210 heat days in a year. Many plant breeders are now including this information in their labeling.

Sowing Seeds

A seed is a living thing containing an embryonic plant and some stored energy. Warmth and moisture are the triggers to start it growing. Use correctly stored seeds, and following the package instructions, you should be able to grow them successfully.

Buying

Seeds ordered direct from a mail-order supplier or purchased in early spring from a store should be fresh and correctly stored. The date on the package will tell you when the seeds were packed and by what date you should use them. Seeds in sealed foil packages should keep for a few years, but those in paper packages should be used within the year.

Storing

Keep the seeds cool and dry until you are ready to sow them. Once the package is open, use seeds of lettuce, carrots, parsnips, and onions during the year because the quality will deteriorate rapidly. However, seeds of cabbages and their relatives, tomatoes, peppers, eggplant, and all members of the cucumber family, will store well. As soon as you've sown what you need, reseal the packet and put it in an airtight container with a bag of silica gel. Keep the container in a cool place, such as a cabinet or the vegetable section in the refrigerator.

When to Sow

Before sowing, make sure the soil is moist and warm enough—but not too warm because 86°F (30°C) and above is too hot for most seeds to germinate. Although the calendar month is a guide to when you can start sowing, you should measure the soil temperature with a soil thermometer to be more accurate. Check the temperature in early morning by pushing the probe into the soil to the same depth as you will sow the seeds. When the soil temperature reaches the minimum germination temperature needed by the seeds for several days at a time, you can sow the seeds.

Preparing a Seedbed

If you haven't dug or tilled the soil the previous fall, use a garden fork to loosen the soil, breaking up any large clumps with the back of the fork. Using a rake, work back and forth to break the surface down into a fine texture, known as a tilth. Do this even if you broke up the soil in fall. Also, rake off any stones or debris until the soil is smooth and level.

Large seeds are easy to handle.

Seed Terms Explained

F1 Hybrid
Seeds produced by the crossing of distinct parent plants. They grow into plants uniform in size and appearance, tend to be vigorous, and produce a good harvest.

Open-Pollinated Varieties
These are seeds from plants that have been pollinated naturally, so there can be a lot of variation in the plants; however, they can be harvested over a longer period.

Heirloom Varieties
These are seeds that have been around for a long time, sometimes kept going by gardening enthusiasts. Many are just good, reliable types that have stood the test of time.

All-American Selection Winners
Each year, trials of new types are conducted all over the country, and the winners are those judged to be distinct improvements over existing cultivars and varieties. Recent winners are worth considering.

Days to Mature
Some cultivars mature more quickly than others. As a rough guide, seed suppliers quote the number of days from when the seeds are sown to when the plants are ready to be harvested or the days from transplanting to harvest. The actual time depends on where you live and the weather.

Use a rake to help prepare a fine tilth in a seedbed.

Use a hoe held on an angle to create a seed furrow.

Let water soak into the bottom of the furrow before sowing seeds.

Sowing Seeds

Sowing in Rows

Most vegetables are sown in rows so the seedlings appear in straight lines and are then easy to tell apart from any weed seedlings—and it is easier to hoe between straight rows. Make a furrow—a shallow V-shape or flat-bottom trench in the soil—using the corner of a hoe or the edge of a piece of lumber pressed into the soil to the correct depth. For long rows, use a piece of string held taut between two stakes to mark the line and run the furrow along it. Space the rows the ideal distance apart for the particular vegetables. If the soil is dry, add water to the bottom of the furrow and let it soak in before sowing.

In a raised bed, seeds are easier to sow in short rows across the width of the bed.

For small seeds, tip some seeds into the palm of your hand and, taking a pinch between your other index finger and thumb, scatter them thinly along a section of the furrow. Cover the seeds by hoeing dry soil over the furrow. Larger seeds, such as squash and bean, are easy to place the correct distance apart. You can either sow two or three seeds together, removing the weaker seedlings later, or sow the seeds at half the final spacing recommended, thinning any extra seedlings.

Double Sowing

Peas and bush bean seeds are often sown in double or triple rows about an inch (2.5cm) or two (5cm) apart, with wider paths for picking. This is also a useful technique for radishes, scallions, and baby leaf salad greens. Use a hoe with a blade 4 to 6 inches (10 to 15cm) wide and make a wide, shallow furrow. Water the furrow if the soil is dry; then scatter the seeds as thinly and evenly as you can across its width. Cover the furrow and lightly firm the surface with the back of a rake.

Hill Sowing

Large, heat-loving plants, such as cucumber,

melon, and squash, will benefit from a method known as hilling, where the seeds are planted in a small hill, or mound, of soil. This hill protects the neck of these plants from rotting. Dig a hole or a trench; then add a bucketful of compost per planting position, and mix it into the soil and water. Hoe the excavated soil and loose soil from between the hills or rows to create a mound up to 12 inches (30cm) high and the same across. Plant two or three seeds into each position. To encourage roots to spread, water the surrounding soil, not the hill, in dry weather.

Minimum Sowing Temperatures

Lettuce will germinate poorly at temperatures above 70°F (21°C). These are minimum temperatures for other plants.

- **40°F (5°C)** All the leafy cabbage family, including Asian greens, fava bean, lettuce, pea, radish, rutabaga, turnip
- **45°F (7°C)** Beet, carrot, leek, onions, parsnip, Swiss chard
- **50°F (10°C)** Celeriac, celery
- **55°F (13°C)** Bush, pole, and runner beans, cucumber, squash, sweet corn, tomato
- **65°F (18°C)** Eggplant, pepper, okra (in cool areas, start these indoors)

Transplants, Bulbs, and Tubers

Some crops are best started in pots indoors and then transplanted in the garden later. If you want only a few plants, buy started plants instead of growing from seeds. Not all vegetables begin from seeds—some are grown from tubers or bulbs.

Why Transplants?

Vegetables that are attacked by soil pests or diseases will get a better start in a pot, and it is easier to protect young plants from slugs and snails, rodents, or birds if grown indoors instead of in the open garden. Large vegetable plants that are slow to start are best transplanted when they are bigger and need their allocated space. Tender plants that need a long growing season to fruit can be started off earlier under glass, which is worthwhile in northern regions with a cold spring.

Starting Transplants

To start vegetable seeds indoors, use a good-quality seed-starting mix because it will be free of disease and weed seeds. You can use any clean container for starting seeds, provided it has drainage holes in the bottom. Keep the pots small to produce compact root systems and stocky seedlings. Use 3-inch (7.5cm) pots for vegetables that grow fast or remain in the pots for more than four weeks. For other plants, 1½–2 inches (4–5cm) is best. If you raise a lot of seedlings, buy plastic seed-starting trays divided into individual cells.

Tender plants germinate and grow best when the temperature is at least 70°F (21°C). These are cucumber, eggplant, melon, okra, pepper, squash, tomato, and tomatillo. You can provide this temperature on a table near a well-lit windowsill in a heated room, but avoid placing the seedlings in direct sunlight because they will scorch. Or grow them in a basement or garage under fluorescent lights hung from chains about 3

Buying started plants saves both time and effort.

inches (7.5cm) above the plants.

All you need for hardy plants, such as members of the cabbage family, celery, leek, lettuce, and onions, is a frost-free place with good light, such as a porch or cold frame. These plants grow rapidly and can be planted outdoors after four weeks.

Hardening Off

When the seedlings have a couple of pairs of true leaves and have more or less filled their pots with roots, it's time to start getting them used to

Sow large seeds in individual containers.

outdoor conditions. Choose a settled period when frosts are no longer predicted in your area. Put the plants in their pots outdoors during the day, and bring them back in at night. Leave them outside for longer each day until they can stay outdoors all night. After about a week or so, your transplants should be ready for planting in the ground outside.

Caring For Started Plants

The following vegetables are worth buying as started plants: cabbage, cauliflower, eggplant, leek, melon, onion, pepper, squash, and tomato. Perennial plants, such as artichokes, asparagus, and rhubarb, are quicker to get started from plants or semi-dried roots or tubers. When you get your started plants home, check the local weather forecast. A calm spell of mild weather is ideal for planting hardy plants; wait for an average temperature of at least 60°F (16°C) before planting tender vegetables. If conditions are not ideal, keep the plants somewhere sheltered and well lit. Water regularly to keep the mix moist but not wet. If you can't plant outdoors for a few weeks, give the plants a little diluted plant food, and make sure you harden off the plants before planting outside.

Planting Outdoors

For transplants and started plants, you do not need a perfect seedbed. Just hoe off any weeds, and scrape back any mulch. Dig a small hole, using a trowel or large dibble at the required spacing, and plant. Tap the top of the pot gently to release the plant with its root ball intact. To release the root balls from divided trays, push a pencil through its drainage hole. Don't pull on the plant.

Place most plants at the same level they were in the pot. However, plant members of the cabbage family deeper so that the first pair of leaves rests on the soil. Plant tomato plants deeply, too, and any buried stem will sprout additional roots. Plant members of the cucumber family so that the top of the root ball is level

or slightly above the soil surface.

Make sure the soil is moist to encourage the roots to search for water and nutrients. In dry weather, water the surrounding soil often, until the plants are growing well. Keep the soil free of weeds by mulching with organic matter or straw, which will also help retain moisture in the soil. Plant widely spaced transplants through a plastic sheet, which is more effective at suppressing weeds, warming the soil, and preventing moisture loss. In case of a cold snap, keep floating row covers handy.

Bulbs and Tubers

Potatoes are sold as "seed" tubers in garden centers or as budded eyes (pieces of tubers with one eye or sprout) by mail-order. Seed tubers are guaranteed free of major diseases, so do not use ordinary potatoes. Make sure tubers are free from rot and are an even size with healthy sprouts starting to form.

Sweet potatoes are sold as "slips," which are rooted shoots. Put them in a jar of water or a pot of soil to prevent them from drying out until

you are ready to plant them.

Onions can be bought as "sets," small, dry bulbs raised from seeds. They are ready to grow to full size when planted in the spring. Garlic is available only as bulbs. Keep the bulbs intact until planting; only then, separate them into individual cloves. Shallots are also sold as bulbs. Check the packages and reject any with soft, shriveled, or rotten bulbs.

Use a plank of wood or string to plant a straight row of transplants.

Selecting Started Vegetable Plants

When you buy started plants, you have the advantage of being able to examine the plants before making your selection. Consider the following:

- Avoid any plants if there has been a frost in the area. If you live in an area prone to late frosts, don't be tempted to buy plants too early—wait until they can go straight outdoors.
- Look for stocky plants with bright green leaves, and avoid plants that have been allowed to dry out. Reject any that are pale or thin and look unhealthy.
- Check that the pots are full of healthy roots—they should not be crowded or "pot-bound."
- Make sure you aren't bringing any pests with your started plant into your garden.

Tender tomato plants are a good choice when buying started plants.

Planting Strategies

It makes sense to use your vegetable garden space efficiently and extend the harvest time as much as possible.

Intercropping

By matching an early crop, such as peas, and a late one, such as bush beans or sweet corn, you can grow two crops in the same space. In early spring, while you wait for the soil to warm up for tender crops, such as squash, tomatoes, and sweet corn, use this space to sneak in an early crop. Leave space between them to plant the main crop. Clear the early crop before the next one needs the space.

Many large vegetables are spaced wide apart, yet they do not use their allocated space for weeks or months. You can use the space between them for a quick crop that will be harvested before the later crop needs the space. Consider choosing a related crop to maintain a crop-rotation plan (See "Crop Families," opposite.) Plant kale, sprouting broccoli, and Brussels sprouts, for example, with kohlrabi, turnip, or radish planted between them. Other examples include scallions between rows of leeks; baby carrots between parsnip and lettuce; or other salad greens around tepees of pole beans. Sweet corn is a good choice for inter-cropping because even when fully grown, the plants don't shade the soil beneath. Try underplanting with pumpkins or bush beans.

Successional Sowing

Many vegetables produce crops over a short period, leading to a glut, followed by nothing. The answer is to make a number of sowings to extend the harvest period. Sow small amounts of lettuce, other salad greens, spinach, radish, and scallions often. Sow short rows a couple of weeks apart, growing just enough to harvest over a week or two—say, two short rows across a raised bed. The same applies for baby carrots, beets, or turnips; make several sowings from spring to fall. Bush beans and peas can be difficult to keep up with once they start producing pods, so sow shorter rows several times through the summer, with the last one timed to finish before the first frosts.

For broccoli and cauliflower, spread the harvest by sow-ing a few seeds or buying a few started plants at a time. Even vegetables that produce a harvest over a long period, such as pole beans and summer squash, can start to tire by late summer, so make a second sowing in midsummer to harvest late summer into fall.

Crop Rotation

The theory is that you should grow annual vegetables that require similar conditions to thrive or that are attacked by the same soil pests or diseases together in the same part of the vegetable garden. You should move these groups around in a specific order each year so that they occupy the same part of the garden only every three or four years. The major benefits are:
• Different vegetables grow roots at different levels and use different quantities of nutrients from the soil, so moving them around will be less draining on the soil.

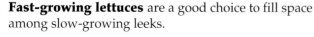

Fast-growing lettuces are a good choice to fill space among slow-growing leeks.

Fillers and Intercrops

These quick-growing plants can fill any gaps that appear as you harvest, or grow them between slower growing crops.

- **Arugula** 6 weeks (as baby leaf)
- **Bean, bush** 10 weeks (not hardy)
- **Beet** 8 weeks (for baby beet)
- **Bok choy** 6–8 weeks
- **Carrot** 10 weeks (early cultivars)
- **Chinese cabbage** 10 weeks
- **Lettuce** 10 weeks (6 weeks for baby leaf)
- **Mustard greens** 4–6 weeks (as baby leaf)
- **Pea** 10 weeks
- **Radish** 4–6 weeks
- **Scallion** 8 weeks
- **Spinach** 6 weeks
- **Turnip** 6–8 weeks

• You can concentrate resources, such as organic matter and fertilizer, on the groups that benefit most.

• Soil diseases and pests won't be able to build up to harmful levels.

• You can reduce damage by insect pests, such as cucumber or flea beetle, that overwinter beneath the crops they attack.

Remember that a crop rotation plan will not prevent diseases that are airborne or spread by crawling insects, flying pests, or slugs.

Divide the crops you plan to grow into their family groups, and assign each family to one of four areas (See "Crop Families," left.) You'll have to combine some of the families; for example, potatoes and roots, the pea and carrot families, and the pea and onion families. Next year, move each group to the next space, with the light feeders taking over from the previous year's heavy feeders.

Adapt the system to suit your needs. If all else fails, try to keep the potato, onion, and cabbage families moving on a three- or four-year cycle and do your best with the rest.

Crop Families

Here are some family groupings that can be grown together.

Cabbage family
Bok choy, broccoli, Brussels sprouts, cabbage, cauliflower, Chinese cabbage and other Asian greens, kale, kohlrabi, rutabaga, and turnip; also arugula and radish

Onion family
Garlic, leek, onions, scallion, shallot

Potato family
Eggplant, pepper, potato, tomatillo, tomato

Carrot family
Carrot, celeriac, celery, fennel, parsley, parsnip

Pea family
Bush, fava, pole, runner, and soy beans, peas; many cover crops, such as alfalfa

Cucumber family
Cucumber, melon, pumpkin, summer and winter squash

Unrelated crops
Plant beets, chicory, lettuce, okra, spinach, sweet corn, sweet potato, Swiss chard wherever there is space. Try to keep heavy and light feeders together.

Extending the Season

In areas with a short growing season, you can gain a couple of extra weeks at the start and end of the summer by using hot caps for individual plants or floating row covers to protect rows of crops from wet or cold or to warm the soil before sowing. The best options are inexpensive row covers made from a sheet of clear plastic and metal hoops. Hitch the sides up to allow ventilation during the day and for watering. Floating row covers made from perforated plastic sheet or spun plastic fibers let light, air, and rain through but keep the temperature inside a few degrees higher than outside. Anchor the edges, but leave the material slack—the plants will lift it as they grow. Add extra layers when frost is forecast.

Separate beds of different vegetables will help make crop rotation easier to follow.

A spun plastic floating row cover will protect the vegetables.

Watering and Feeding

In most parts of the country, there should be plenty of moisture and nutrients in the soil to start with in early spring, but as the growing season progresses you may need to supplement what is there. For example, unless there's an inch (2.5cm) of rain a week, the initial water reserve will diminish. You'll need to add about half a gallon per square foot (1.8L per 10cm²) a week (and more at higher temperatures) to make up the difference.

Watering Efficiently

Even if the ground surface is dust dry, the soil may be moist farther down—dig a hole to check. Watering little and often can do more harm than good, so instead apply a week's water once a week so it soaks in. Always water in newly transplanted vegetables and seedbeds as the seedlings are emerging unless it has rained. Once plants are established, concentrate on watering plants that are almost ready to be harvested or on those that need to grow fast to produce tender leaves or stems, such as lettuce.

Conserving Water

In an arid area or one that has droughts, water conservation is vital. Place rainwater barrels to collect runoff from roofs to use in the garden. Improve your soil structure by adding organic matter, such as mulches. Target water on the crops that benefit most and at the stage in their life cycle that will produce the biggest yields. Water the soil, not the

A garden hose is a popular choice for spot watering of plants.

What to Water and When

Leafy crops
- **Broccoli and cauliflower** Water transplants and when the heads start to form.
- **Cabbage** Water transplants and when the heads start to form; do not water when heads are fully formed.
- **Lettuce, Asian greens, and other greens** Water throughout their life.

Root crops
- **Quick-growing baby crops** Water beet, carrot, radish, and turnip baby crops continuously.
- **Leek** Water both seedlings or transplants until cooler fall weather.
- **Onions** Water when the bulbs start to form; stop when they start to ripen.
- **Pea and bean** Water when flowers appear and while pods are forming.
- **Potato** Water early crops throughout growth, the later crops when in flower.

Fruit-Bearing Vegetables
- **Cucumber, melon, summer, and winter squash** Water when the first fruit forms until harvest.
- **Eggplant, pepper, and tomato** Water regularly when the fruit starts to form until harvest.

Dripper systems can cater to the needs of individual plants.

plants, and water when it is cool to minimize evaporation. Get water directly to the roots by using plastic soda bottles or milk containers. Punch a small hole in the lid, and cut the bottom. Bury these halfway in the soil next to widely spaced plants, such as cucumbers, melons, squash, and tomatoes. In a small garden, you can use a 2-gallon (7.5L) watering can.

Irrigation Systems

There are two types of drip irrigation system. Soaker hoses are made from porous rubber that leaks water slowly along their length. Run these along rows of plants; link several lengths together with T-joints; and connect them to your outside faucet. Dripper systems use a number of fine tubes that connect to a hose running around the vegetable garden. Each tube ends in a water emitter, or dripper, which is adjustable to suit the needs of different plants. Once either of these systems is set up, you can water the whole garden or sections of it simply by turning on the faucet for a set period of time. Add an automatic water timer if you are away a lot.

Nutrients

There are a few main plant nutrients that your vegetables will need to flourish. Vegetables need varying amounts of nitrogen, which is good for leaf growth. Reliable sources include dried blood, fish meal, and animal manures. Nitrates are soluble, so they need to be replenished each season. Potassium, or potash, is needed for flower and fruit production, while phosphorous is important for building strong root systems.

Plants also need trace nutrients in smaller quantities—magnesium and manganese, for example. Most of the others can be supplied by regular additions of compost or manure, or by using a tonic, such as a kelp meal or fish emulsion.

Fertilizer Types

Fertilizers supply the same nutrients as organic matter, but more quickly. They are useful if you cannot provide enough bulky organic matter or to help boost greedier crops. Check the label for the nutrient analysis. Organic fertilizers are often preferred by gardeners, but there are also man-made artificial products that contain known amounts of the three major nutrients. A balanced fertilizer (with equal percentages of all three) is good for most vegetables. Slow-release fertilizers release their nutrients over a period and are particularly useful for containers. Switch to a liquid potash fertilizer when fruiting vegetables, such as tomatoes, start to produce fruit.

A well-used plot may benefit from an application of fertilizer.

Potatoes need a lot of nitrogen.

Nutrient Requirements

Crops with a high need for nitrogen include: beet, broccoli, Brussels sprouts, cabbage, cauliflower, Asian greens, leek, potato, spinach, and Swiss chard. Crops with a moderate demand include: asparagus, chicory, eggplant, garlic, lettuce, onion, pepper, squash, sweet corn, and tomato. Carrot, cucumber, fava bean, parsnip, pea, radish, rutabaga, and turnip have a low-nitrogen demand.

Cover Crops

These inedible crops, also known as "green manures," keep the soil covered during periods between crops to prevent soil erosion. Clear the existing crop; roughly loosen the soil surface; scatter the cover crop seeds evenly and thickly; and work them into the soil with a rake. Water thoroughly, especially at the end of a dry summer. To harvest, use a spade to chop the foliage; then dig or rototill the area to bury them and improve the soil for the crops that follow.

Green Manures

Here is a list of plants that are good choices to grow as a green manure.

- **Alfalfa** A legume; sow it in spring.
- **Bean** Field or fava beans are legumes for fall sowing.
- **Buckwheat** A tender crop; sow in spring or summer.
- **Crimson clover** A legume for sowing in fall.
- **Lupin** The field lupin is a legume suitable for sowing in spring.
- **Mustard** A fast-growing crop that you can sow from spring to fall.
- **Rye, annual** Sow in either spring or fall; dig it in before it begins to set seed.
- **Rye, winter** A deep-rooting crop you can sow in fall.

Watering and Feeding

Weeding

Weeds compete with vegetables, especially newly sown or planted ones, for water, nutrients, and space. Perennial weeds survive as deep taproots or underground roots or rhizomes and come back year after year. They can become a real nuisance among fruit or perennial vegetables, so it's best to take time to destroy them before planting. Annual weeds flower and set seed each year. Most soil is full of dormant seeds from annual weeds, and each time you disturb the soil, they will get a chance to germinate.

Mulching

Apart from controlling weeds, mulching—covering the soil surface around and between plants—has a number of other benefits in the vegetable garden. It helps to reduce water evaporating from the soil in hot weather, so there will be less need for watering. It helps to warm up cold soils in the spring by absorbing heat from the sun, and it will keep the soil cooler in summer. Homemade compost is the best mulch of all. It's free and nutritious and the quickest form of recycling you can do. (See "Homemade Garden Compost," page 9.) Other good sources of organic mulches include chopped or shredded fallen leaves, hay or straw, grass clippings, composted animal manures, and bark chips. If you can get these in bulk and for little or no cost, pile them around crops in a 2-inch (5cm) layer.

Sheet Barriers

Clear plastic sheets will help warm the soil in spring, which will produce a flush of weed seedlings. Black plastic sheets will prevent weeds and conserve soil moisture, but they will not warm the soil. Infrared transmitting mulches are green or brown and help warm the soil to stop weeds but are costly. Landscaping fabric is sheeting made from tightly woven plastic fibers that prevents weeds, conserves moisture, and lets water through.

Put plastic sheets in place before the crop is sown or planted. Stretch the material taut, and bury or weigh down the edges. You can leave the sheet in place to control weeds and cut an X in the material just large enough to plant widely spaced vegetables through it.

Use a hoe to remove small weeds near your plants.

You can plant transplants through slits made in a black plastic sheet, which will suppress weeds.

Weeding Methods

- Mulch with organic matter to prevent annual weeds.
- If possible, cover an area for at least a year with a black plastic sheet to clear it of weeds before you start cultivating it.
- Cover the soil in early spring with a clear plastic sheet. This will warm the soil and bring up a flush of weed seedlings, which you can hoe off.
- Hoe regularly between rows of crops. Choose a warm, dry day so that hoed weeds will shrivel up and die quickly. Keep the blade parallel with the soil surface or just below it, and aim to sever the weeds neatly from their roots—keep the hoe blade sharp.
- Hand-weed among rows of vegetables where hoeing will cause too much damage to the plants. Combine it with thinning seedlings until the plants overshadow any new weeds, blocking sunlight.
- Weed killers are best kept out of the vegetable garden. The one exception is to use a systemic weed killer to kill the roots of perennial weeds before you lay out the garden.

Weeding

Supporting

Some vegetables and fruits are climbers, and others may require support in exposed gardens. With all support systems, erect them before you sow or plant the vegetables. This will avoid damaging the crops while they are growing.

Annual Supports

Climbing vegetables, such as the pole bean, need something to climb.

• Tepees are groups of poles—bamboo poles are best—arranged in a circle and tied together at the top. The circle should be 2–3 feet (60–90cm) wide and the highest point 6–7 feet (1.8–2.1m) high, so you'll need 8-foot (2.4m) poles. Make sure you push them well into the soil so they don't topple over.

• Make a trellis frame to support rows of climbers. You can make the structure out of bamboo poles, although windy areas require additional bracing. Start with two rows of poles, with each pair tied together at the top; then strengthen with horizontal poles positioned across the top of the tied-together poles. Once you've made the frame, attach vertical strings at 6-inch (15cm) intervals for the beans to climb.

• Or use stout posts at each end of the row. Run strong wires between these, and tie vertical bamboo poles, strings, light wire, or plastic mesh to them. Vine crops, such as cucumber, melon, and small-fruited squash climb using tendrils rather than by twining, so horizontal strings or plastic mesh will help support them.

• You can train indeterminate tomatoes with a single stem and no side shoots. They need to be tied to a single stake per plant or a trellis of bamboo poles for rows of plants.

Caging

Tomato plants that are not trained as a single stem can become unruly. Grow them inside store-bought tomato cages, or better still, make your own from a square of concrete reinforcing mesh with a 6-inch (15cm) grid. Roll it into a cylinder 2 feet (60cm) in diameter and about 4–5 feet (1.2–1.5m) tall, and push it into the ground around the plants.

Tepees are ideal supports for beans and peas.

To tie a stem to a support, use a soft material, such as garden twine.

Staking

Taller vegetables, such as asparagus and Jerusalem artichokes, may need support. If needed, hammer stakes to support each plant or set up pairs of stakes along the rows and surround the row with string. Other crops that might need support include peas, beans, eggplant, peppers, and sprouting broccoli.

Permanent Support

Berry-producing fruits are a long-term investment, and grape vines even more so. It is well worth building a strong structure to support them. Use stout posts at least 3 inches (7.5cm) across made from durable lumber, or treat the part that is to go in the ground with a nontoxic wood preservative. The posts should be at least 5 feet (1.5m) tall aboveground and extend 2 feet (60cm) below it. Space the posts 6–8 feet (1.8–2.4m) apart, and add diagonal planks and braces at the ends for strength. Nail strong wire around the outside of each post at the top and another halfway up so that the wires are parallel on each side.

Supporting

Pest and Disease Control

Netting is just one form of protection for vegetables.

Pest and Disease Control

Keeping your plants healthy is the best approach to avoiding diseases. Once a plant has been infected by a disease, there's not a great deal you can do about it, so preventive measures are the best solution.

Garden Hygiene

When plants show the first symptoms of diseases, such as potato blight or mildew, pick off the affected leaves or shoots. If a plant is beyond saving, pull it up and you may prevent the disease from spreading. Dispose of any diseased plants and debris, including fallen leaves, in the trash. At the end of the season, gather all healthy crop remains—nothing that is disease ridden—and add them to the compost pile.

Clean Seeds

Always buy seeds, seed potatoes, sweet potato slips, and onion and garlic sets from a reputable source. Be careful if you save your own seeds—make sure you take them from the healthiest-looking plants, and reject any seedlings that aren't growing normally.

Air and Water

Diseases such as powdery and downy mildews are made worse by humid conditions, so always give plants plenty of room, especially in late summer, to allow air circulation and prevent them from developing these conditions. Other diseases, such as blight, are spread by splashing rain. Keep the foliage dry by watering the soil—not the plants.

Crop Rotation

Crop rotation can prevent soil diseases from building up to damaging levels. (See page 16.) If any plant develops a soil disease, destroy the remains of that plant and grow vegetables in the same family in a different part of the garden.

Resistant Plants

If your crops regularly develop a particular disease, check the seed brochures for resistant types. Or look for "tolerant" cultivars that do well in your area—they will be less susceptible to disease.

Virus Diseases

Diseases caused by a virus are difficult to control and are often spread by sap-feeding insects, so keep aphids off your plants.

Fungicides

These simple substances can be used as preventive measures:
• Dissolve 1 tablespoon of baking soda plus 1 tablespoon of vegetable oil in a cup (225ml) of warm water; then add to a gallon (3.8L) of water as a spray for powdery mildew.
• Compost tea, a stimulant made by leaving a bucketful of compost or well-rotted manure in a barrel of water for four days before draining, is used by many gardeners as a disease preventive.
• Copper, a spray of copper sulfate or Bordeaux mixture, helps control damping off in seedlings, blight, and gray mold.
• Sulfur can help control powdery mildew, black spot, scab, and some other fungal diseases.

A floating row cover is easy to set up over plants—and easy to remove.

Ladybugs can help to keep vegetable plants free from aphids.

Caterpillar droppings are a sure sign of insect problems.

Slugs and snails can munch through your vegetables in no time.

Preventing Pests

Pests come in many forms, from hungry deer to minute spider mites. If you wait for them to strike, there may be little you can do. However, if you prepare your defenses in advance, you can outwit most of them.

Fences

The only real defense against larger pests, such as deer and rabbits, is to erect a wire fence surrounding the vegetable garden. Make sure this is high enough so that larger animals cannot jump over it, and bury the bottom to deter rabbits.

Nets and Covers

For birds and larger insects, such as cabbage butterflies, the best protection is to cover beds with netting—match the mesh size to the pest you want to keep out. Use hoops to support the net well above the crop, and secure the edges all around. This will work well for strawberries, but for larger fruiting plants you may need to construct a taller wooden frame or cage to support the mesh.

Floating row covers are made from spun plastic with such tiny holes that even the smallest insects cannot get through, although air and water can. Lay it loosely over a crop, and weigh down the edges to prevent insects from getting underneath. Loosen the edges as the crop grows. Lift the cover for weeding in the evening, when insects are less active. Remove the cover when fruit-bearing crops, such as squash, start to flower to allow pollinators in, when the pests

are no longer a threat, when you start harvesting, or in hot weather, when plants may scorch.

Handpicking and Traps

Pick off larger leaf pests, such as cabbage worms and beetles, and put them on a bird table to attract birds to feed on them. Use upturned pots, pieces of lumber, or damp burlap around the vegetable garden to attract slugs or snails and destroy them. Alternatively, bury a plastic cup or metal can so the lip is level with the soil surface. Fill the container with beer; leave it overnight; and collect the drowned creatures each day.

Collars and Barriers

Protect young plants from slugs and cutworms by surrounding each plant with a collar made from 4–6-inch (10–15cm) open-ended sections cut from plastic beverage bottles. Protect raised beds and containers with a continuous band of copper tape. Collars that are made from thick, black plastic will help protect young cabbage family plants from cabbage root maggots.

Attracting Predators

Encourage insects, spiders, and other creatures that feed on aphids and other pests. A patch of weeds in a corner of the garden, a pile of rotting logs, or a compost pile will harbor beetles and spiders. Mix a few bright, open flowers into the vegetable garden to attract hover flies, which eat aphids. Lacewings are attracted to carrot-family flowers, such as fennel, and both they and

their larvae eat aphids. Provide nesting sites and fresh water for birds and a pond for toads and frogs, all of which will eat insects.

Insecticides

These are the last resort if pests get out of control and should be used with care. Here are some natural insecticides that you can try:
• *Bacillus thuringiensis* (Bt for short) kills caterpillars; another type kills Colorado potato beetle grubs.
• Garlic and pepper sprays repel small insect pests, such as aphids, mites, and leafhoppers.
• Horticultural oil and insecticidal soap kills soft-bodied insects, such as aphids and caterpillars.
• Milky spores kill the underground grubs of Japanese beetles.
• Neem oil stops leaf-eating pests.
• Pyrethrum kills many pests on contact but breaks down rapidly.

Before using a pesticide, always carefully read the label and follow any precautions. Spray on a warm, calm day; early evening is better because beneficial insects are less active. Cover the undersides of leaves and growing tips thoroughly.

Harvesting and Storing

The secret for the best vegetables and fruit is to pick little and often, eating them on the same day that you harvest them. However, even with careful planning, a glut of some vegetables at certain times is often unavoidable. This is not a problem, because most vegetables, herbs, and fruit can be stored or preserved for use in winter.

Deciding When to Pick

Each vegetable has a period when it is at its best. Some have a relatively short window and, if you miss it, the produce will spoil. However, others have a much longer season and you can pick them anytime up to full maturity. Refer to the individual vegetable entries for specific advice.

Harvesting Methods

The ideal time to pick most fresh crops is early in the morning, when they are cool and fresh. Use a sharp knife to harvest a leafy crop, especially heading lettuces and cabbages. Cut individual leaves from leaf lettuce and other leafy greens, kale, Swiss chard, or spinach.

You can handpick vegetables that are the fruit of the plant, such as tomatoes. Make sure you avoid damage to the plant as you harvest them because any opened areas can be an entry point for disease. When you handpick, hold the stem in one hand as you pull with the other. Cut peppers, eggplant, cucumbers, and zucchini with a short piece of stem attached, using a knife or pruning shears. For tomatoes, keep the green calyx attached, which should come away with the fruit if you snap the stem at the "knuckle." Cut winter squash at the stem just below the bottom of the fruit.

Use a garden fork to loosen root vegetables, but avoid spearing them with the fork's prongs. For potatoes and Jerusalem artichokes, use the fork to first loosen the soil, but then

When cutting tough plants, such as Swiss chard, use a sharp knife.

Snap or cut off Brussels sprouts, working from the bottom up.

use your hands to collect the crop. Long-root crops, such as carrots and parsnips, will require you to push the fork down to a good depth before lifting. Leeks, celery, and onions can also be lifted with a fork.

Storage Methods

If you can't use the produce shortly after picking it, use one of these storage methods to preserve it:

Short-term storage: Vegetables will usually stay fresh for a few days or a week in the refrigerator. Put leafy greens in unsealed plastic bags to stop them from wilting. Don't wash the vegetables until just before you cook or serve them.

Freezing: This is a good way to preserve extra vegetables, such as asparagus, broccoli, bush beans, baby carrots, cauliflower, peas, spinach, tomatoes, and zucchini, and berries, such as blueberries, currants, and raspberries. Most vegetables will need to be blanched (plunged into

boiling water) and cooled rapidly to preserve their flavor before freezing. Fresh chopped herbs and chili peppers can be frozen easily by packing them into ice-cube trays.

Drying: Most herbs can be picked when mature—just before they start to flower is the best time—and hung up in bunches to dry. Pick on a hot day, and hang in a warm, dry, airy place to dry off completely. Fully ripe chili peppers can be dried. Hang up the whole plant in a warm, airy place until the fruit is leathery.

Storing indoors: You can store root vegetables dug up during the late fall in a cool place indoors. These include potatoes, sweet potatoes, carrots, beets, rutabaga, and parsnips. Make sure the potatoes are dry—lay them in a dry, airy place indoors—and remove any damaged tubers; then store them in the dark. Store beets, carrots, parsnips, and rutabaga in deep wooden boxes containing moist sand. Start with an inch (2.5cm) of sand—this should be just moist, not wet. Lay a single layer of roots on the sand so they are not touching. Add more sand until all the roots are covered; then repeat with more layers until the box is full.

Onions, garlic, and shallots can be stored in a dry place with good ventilation. Check them often, and discard any soft or sprouted bulbs. Pumpkins and winter squash will keep in a cool, dry basement or garage. They don't need to be kept in the dark. Check regularly; discard any fruit that become soft.

Leaving the crop outdoors: In milder areas, you can leave certain types of vegetables in the garden until you eat them. Kale and Brussels sprouts will cope with moderate frosts. Carrots and parsnips can be left in their rows over winter; cover the row with straw or leaves.

Seed crops: Some plants, including beans, popcorn, and sunflower (edible types), are grown for their dry seeds. Leave the plants to dry in the sun; then shake out the dry seeds. Store them in airtight jars.

Leave beets in the ground until you are ready to use them.

Harvesting and Storing

Storage Strategies and Good Yields

Below are the average yields of vegetables and the storage methods that you can use for them.

	YIELD 1 FT/30CM ROW	YIELD PER PLANT	FREEZE	DRY	STORE INDOORS	LEAVE IN GARDEN*
■ **Asparagus**	1 lb. (450g)		•			
■ **Bean, bush**	1 lb. (450g)		•	•		
■ **Bean, pole**	1½–2 lb. (680–900g)		•	•		
■ **Beet**	1½–2 lb. (680–900g)				•	•
■ **Broccoli**		1 lb. (450g)	•			
■ **Brussels sprouts**		1½ lb. (680g)	•			•
■ **Cabbage**		5–6 lb. (2.3–2.7kg)				•
■ **Carrot**	1½ lb. (680g)		•		•	•
■ **Cauliflower**		2–3 lb. (900g–1.4kg)	•			
■ **Celery**	1½–2 lb. (680–900g)					•
■ **Corn, sweet**		1–2 cobs	•			
■ **Cucumber***		3 lb. (1.4kg)				
■ **Eggplant**		2 lb. (900g)	•			
■ **Kale**		1–2 lb. (450–900g)				•
■ **Leek**	2 lb. (900g)					•
■ **Melon**		4–6 lb. (1.8–2.7kg)	•			
■ **Okra**		1–2 lb. (450–900g)	•			
■ **Onion**	1 lb. (450g)				•	
■ **Parsnip**	1½–2 lb. (680–900g)				•	•
■ **Pea, snow**	1½–2 lb. (680–900g)		•			
■ **Pepper**		1–2 lb. (450–900g)	•	•		
■ **Potato**		5–6 lb. (2.3–2.7kg)			•	
■ **Spinach and Swiss chard**	1½–2 lb. (680–900g)		•			
■ **Squash, summer**		5–6 lb. (2.3–2.7kg)	•			
■ **Squash, winter**		8–9 lb. (3.6–4kg)			•	
■ **Tomato**		4–5 lb. (1.8–2.3kg)	•	•		
■ **Turnip**	1–1½ lb. (450–680g)				•	•

*Not usually stored, but smaller types can be pickled.

part 2

growing vegetables

You are now ready to decide what to grow in your garden. Growing vegetables can be somewhat unpredictable. The type of seeds or plants you select, the local weather, and the condition of the soil in your garden all come into play. Fortunately, you'll find the information you need on the following pages. You'll learn when it is best to sow and harvest each one of the vegetables, fruits, and herbs covered. The listings include guidelines for caring for your crop and how to deal with common pests. For other information, such as the frost dates in your area, you can contact your local Cooperative Extension Service.

Salad greens and other leafy vegetables

Leafy vegetables lose water almost as soon as they are picked, so freshness is key for taste, texture, and vitamins. Even if you grow only a limited range of edible plants, a selection of salad and other leafy greens is vital because you will have far superior produce to anything you can buy. Most salad greens are quick growing and do not put down deep roots, so any container or shallow raised bed is ideal. The cabbage family takes a bit more commitment, but it is worth growing your family favorites, especially those ready to harvest in winter.

Roots, tubers, and fruits

Nature stores plant energy in roots and tubers, so vegetables such as potatoes, carrots, and beets provide hearty, nutritious meals, whether eaten fresh or stored. Then there are the prolific producers—members of the cucumber family and the legumes that will keep you supplied all summer, along with hot peppers and chilies and tomatoes. Finally, the pleasure of eating fruits—from sweet juicy strawberries to plump grapes—freshly harvested from plants needs no introduction.

Don't forget herbs

The flavor and appearance of fresh herbs can lift a dish from the ordinary to the memorable, and the great bonus of growing your own supply of herbs is that you can use generous handfuls at their peak of flavor. So while the quantities used may be small, the difference herbs make to the taste and presentation of your dishes will be outstanding. Those started from seeds, such as cilantro and parsley, can be grown in containers or in rows in beds, while perennial herbs, such as sage and rosemary, will easily fit into ornamental borders.

Arugula

A quick grower with a lively peppery flavor

Add zest to your salads by mixing arugula with other salad greens. Wild (or rustic) arugula has narrow, finely divided leaves. Salad, or cultivated, arugula is bulkier, grows quicker, and has a mild flavor.

When to sow: Year-round, except summer in hot regions.

How to sow: Sow seeds directly into a well-prepared seedbed. Sow thinly in short rows 6 inches (15cm) apart. Or if your soil is free of annual weeds, broadcast the seeds thinly into small patches. Sow small amounts every two weeks to produce a constant supply of young leaves.

Care: Grow arugula in fertile soil that has had plenty of organic matter worked into it. Water regularly to keep the soil constantly moist, especially during hot spells.

Harvesting: Start cutting as soon as the plants reach 3 inches (8cm) high. Use scissors to cut the plant 1 inch (2.5cm) above soil level, leaving a stump to regrow and produce fresh leaves. Harvest just before you need the leaves for maximum freshness.

Cultivated arugula has rounder leaves than wild arugula.

Endive

A popular European salad green

This bitter green is also grown in North America to add to salads from summer to winter. There are two types of endive: frisée and broad-leaved, or escarole. Their bitter taste adds piquancy to salads.

When to sow: Spring to early summer, or late summer for a winter crop.

How to sow: For loose leaves, sow seeds directly into a well-prepared seedbed in rows; thin to 6 inches (15cm) apart for frisée endive or 12 inches (30cm) for escarole. For large hearts, start the seeds in small pots or divided trays. Sow a few seeds per pot or division; then remove the weakest seedling. Transplant 10 inches (25cm) apart.

Care: Endive is trouble free if the soil is kept moist. Even well-grown endive is too bitter for some tastes, but you can produce paler, sweeter-tasting leaves by blanching them while still in the ground.

Harvesting: Pick leaves as you need them, or cut off a whole head about 1 inch (2.5cm) above ground level. Frost will make the flavor less bitter. Store in plastic bags in the refrigerator for up to ten days.

The outer leaves will be more bitter than the heart.

Chicory

A group of bitter salad greens

Add flavor and color to salads with chicory, a cool-weather leafy green with a bitter flavor. Members of this family include cutting chicory—both rosette and loose-leafed types; the upright head of blanched greens known as Belgian endive; and radicchio, which has a striking red-and-white heart.

When to sow: In spring for an early harvest, or in late summer for a fall harvest. Sow the hearted types, such as radicchio and Belgian endive, in late summer for a late fall or winter crop. Be sure to sow at least three months before the first frost. In mild winter areas, the plants will survive winter without protection.

Radicchio, a form of chicory, will start to turn red in the fall.

How to sow: Sow the seeds of all types directly in rows 12 inches (30cm) apart and ¼ inch (6.5mm) deep. Thin seedlings to 10–12 inches (25–30cm) apart for large hearts or Belgian endive. For cutting chicory, thin the seedlings to 9–10 inches (23–25cm) apart.

Care: Water the soil well in dry periods, or the plants will become too bitter. Mulch with organic matter to retain soil moisture and suppress weeds. Slugs and snails can be a nuisance. If perennial cutting chicory sends up a flower stalk, cut the plant back and it will resprout.

Harvesting: These are hardy plants that will keep in the garden well into winter, especially if protected with a mulch. Pick individual leaves of cutting types as needed when about 4 inches (10cm) high, or cut off whole heads. If you leave the stump, it may regrow to produce fresh leaves. You can leave radicchio in the ground until needed. When the heads feel firm, remove the outer green leaves to reveal the red-and-white hearts. Belgian endive will be ready to harvest about four weeks after forcing it, when the chicon is 6 inches (15cm) high. (See Smart Tip, right.) If you return the pot with the roots to a dark, cool room, it may resprout a second or third time.

Recommended cultivars:
• 'Grumolo' is a cutting type that forms rosettes of dark green leaves (55 days).
• 'Indigo' is a fast-growing, round-headed radicchio cultivar with bright red leaves (72 days).
• 'Sugarloaf', a pale green loose-leaf cutting cultivar, forms a firm heart (55 days).
• 'Witloof' is a Belgian endive type that will produce pale green, upright plants with firm hearts (110 days).

SMART TIP

Winter greens
The roots of chicory relative Belgian endive are dug up in the fall and forced indoors during the winter to produce sprouts. The leaves are grown without exposure to light. Dig up the roots when they are at least 1 inch (2.5cm) wide at the top in late fall and trim to 6–9 inches (15–23cm); cut the leaves 1 inch (2.5cm) from the top. Store the roots in boxes of moist sand. Plant three or four roots at a time in a large pot filled with potting mix so that the cut stumps are just visible. Cover the pot with another upturned pot to exclude all light, and store in a dark, cool place with a temperature of about 50°F (10°C). Belgian endive will be ready to harvest about four weeks after forcing it, when the sprouts are 6 inches (15cm) high.

Lettuce

The ultimate salad green

Lettuce is a quick and easy crop to grow, is ideal for containers, and is decorative enough for the ornamental garden. Growing your own allows you to appreciate it at its freshest.

When to sow: Sow batches of lettuce regularly throughout the year for a succession of crops. Lettuce will germinate erratically when the temperature is above 70°F (21°C), so in warm regions sow in spring and fall. In mild areas, you can sow outside over the winter—select hardy types. In cool areas, you can grow lettuce outside from spring until fall.

How to sow: You can sow seeds directly into a well-prepared seedbed. Sow thinly, about ½ inch (1.3cm) deep, in rows 12 inches (30cm) apart. You can also start seeds in small pots or trays, or buy already-started plants and transplant them. Grow these until they have about four leaves; then plant them outdoors 12 inches (30cm) apart for mature heads, but closer if you intend to pick as loose leaves.

Care: Lettuce requires fertile soil and a good supply of nitrogenous fertilizer. Make sure you water regularly in hot, dry weather to maintain rapid growth. Seedlings and young plants are particularly vulnerable to slugs and snails, so use traps or barriers if necessary.

Allow enough room for lettuce heads to develop.

Harvesting: You can harvest lettuce anytime from the first baby leaves to big firm-hearted plants, so each planting can be used over a long period. Use a sharp knife to cut a head of lettuce just above soil level. Hearting lettuce types, such as butterheads and crispheads, are best left until they produce firm hearts. Check their progress by pressing gently with the back of your hand. Whole-lettuce hearts should keep for at least a week in a refrigerator. Loose-leaf types are best picked and used immediately.

SMART TIP

Preventing brown leaf edges
Leaf edges can turn brown when the plant is suffering from an ailment known as "tip burn." This is caused by calcium deficiency due to sudden hot weather. Keep plants well watered during hot, dry spells. Grow lettuce in semishade in hot climates.

Lettuce is an ideal vegetable for growing in a raised bed.

The butterhead has a round head with soft, buttery textured leaves and yellow hearts. It is best grown late in the season, and doesn't keep well.

The crisphead lettuce is a large plant with crinkled outer leaves and a firm, pale crisp heart. Leave in the ground until the heart is solid.

The Batavia is a type of summer crisp lettuce, but the leaves form a looser heart and have a better flavor. Some cultivars have red leaves.

Recommended cultivars:

There are many types available—from crunchy icebergs to sweet crisp romaines to bright red loose-leaf types.
• Batavian 'Merlot' is a red-leaved Batavian cultivar (50–65 days).
• Butterhead 'Buttercrunch' is a reliable older cultivar (65 days).
• Butterhead 'Cassandra' is a modern cultivar that has been developed with better resistance to fungal diseases (70–85 days).
• Crisphead 'Iceberg' is a reliable older type (75 days).
• 'Great Lakes' produces crisp, tender heads (85 days).
• Loose-leaf 'Lollo Rossa' is a decorative Italian cultivar that has bright red, frilly leaves (55 days).
• Loose-leaf 'Salad Bowl' is a typical green cultivar with deeply indented leaves. There is also a red version (45–50 days).
• Romaine 'Little Gem' forms a small head that is ideal for closer spacing during summer (54 days). 'Chartwell' is a good modern hybrid (54 days).
• Romaine 'Winter Density' is a hardier cultivar for fall sowing and may survive over winter in mild areas.

Romaine is a tall, pointed lettuce with a paler firm heart. It is sweet and crunchy and slow to send up flower stalks.

SMART TIP

Pest control

If your lettuce is growing stunted and crinkled, aphids are the most likely cause. To confirm this, examine the undersides of the leaves and the leaf bases. Spray with an organic pesticide based on pyrethrum or insecticidal soap.

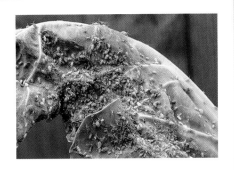

Loose-leaf types, as the name implies, produce a lot of leaves but little in the way of a heart.

Mesclun & Others

A melody of young, tender greens

Instead of using only mature salad-green leaves, you can sow a mix of salad-green seeds and cut the immature leaves as needed. These immature leaves are known as mesclun. The choice is between using prepared-seed mixes or your own combination of seeds using your favorite flavors. Try adding herbs, such as cilantro, basil, or chervil, each with its own distinctive taste.

When to sow: Sow small amounts of seeds about two or three weeks apart from spring until late fall. Avoid sowing during the hottest weather because many of the constituents of a mesclun seed mix will go to seed rapidly or the flavor will become hot or bitter.

How to sow: Mesclun seed mixes are best sown in patches or bands rather than rows. The advantage of buying the seeds separately and creating your own mix is that you can adjust the ratio to produce your ideal mix. However, make sure they have a similar sowing-to-harvest time. Water the furrows thoroughly before sowing; then cover with soil to keep the seeds moist. It is a great crop for containers or raised beds.

Care: Water regularly, especially in hot, dry weather, to keep the soil surface moist at all times. Most of the plant cultivars used in mesclun seed mixes will regrow when cut, and with care you should get three or more crops. Protect the plants from pests, such as slugs and snails.

A mixture of mesclun leaves adds interesting textures and colors to a salad.

Harvesting: Baby leaves can be cut as soon as they grow to about 2 inches (5cm) high; ideally, they should be about 4 inches (10cm) high. Leaves this small will be sweet and subtle. As they get bigger, the flavor of the more exotic types will intensify, so you can adjust the flavor to suit your own taste. Harvest just enough for a meal and serve right away for maximum flavor and freshness. Use sharp scissors to cut the leaves about ½ inch (1.3cm) above soil level, leaving the stumps to regrow. Plunge into a bowl of cold water; rinse thoroughly.

Recommended types and cultivars:
• Arugula adds a distinctive peppery flavor but can outgrow lettuce in the mix. It is also prone to sending up flower stalks in hot weather and is a magnet for flea beetles, which leave small round holes in leaves.
• Corn salad is slow growing and can be overwhelmed by faster-growing leaves in summer, but is worth adding to winter mixes.
• Chicories, including radicchio and endive, add a bitter note, as well as color and texture.
• Kale, such as 'Black Tuscany', or the red types, such as 'Red Russian', are mild and tender as young leaves.
• Loose-leaf lettuce makes a good choice, especially the red kinds that add color and interest.
• Oriental greens, such as bok choy and mizuna, add a mild peppery flavor. Chinese mustards and cress, such as 'Wrinkle Crinkle', add a more distinctive heat to the mix.
• Any type of lettuce can be picked as baby leaves. Try the romaines—they produce sweet, meaty leaves.

When ready to harvest, use scissors to snip the leaves.

Spinach & Swiss Chard

Quick-growing greens

Spinach can be added to salads when harvested as young leaves or cooked as mature leaves. Swiss chard is easier to grow and more colorful. The leaves can be used in the same way as spinach, and the succulent stems make a useful additional vegetable.

When to sow: Early spring or fall for spinach; spring for Swiss chard.

How to sow: Make several sowings of spinach between four and ten weeks before the first fall frost date in your area. Sow spinach ½ inch (1.3cm) deep in rows 12 inches (30cm) apart. The large seeds are easy to handle. Space them 2 inches (5cm) apart. Thin spinach seedlings later to 6 inches (15cm) apart. In cool areas, Swiss chard is best sown in spring, as soon as the soil conditions allow. In warm areas, make several sowings through the spring and summer. Swiss chard "seeds" are actually corky fruit containing several seeds. Like beet, each "seed" will produce a clump of seedlings. You can separate these later, thin them, or leave them to grow as a clump. Sow seeds for Swiss chard as for spinach, but thin the plants in several stages to 12 inches (30cm) apart.

Care: Both crops need moist soil and are greedy feeders. If growth starts to slow down, side-dress with a general-purpose or high-nitrogen fertilizer. Both crops are attractive to slugs and snails—use barriers or traps.

Harvesting: Both spinach and Swiss chard leaves can be eaten raw in salad when small and tender. Cook larger leaves. Pick individual spinach leaves, or cut whole plants. Cut the whole of young Swiss chard plants, but leave a stump, which should regrow. Or cut leaves when they reach 10 inches (25 cm) long, starting from the outside of the plant. Steam or stir-fry the stalks.

Recommended cultivars:
• 'Bright Lights' is a vibrant Swiss chard mix with white, yellow, red, and intermediate-color stems (60 days).
• 'Bright Yellow' is a Swiss chard cultivar with golden yellow stems and green leaves (60 days).

Orach

Also called "mountain spinach," orach is a warm-weather alternative to spinach. It grows rapidly into a large plant, up to 4 feet (1.2m) high, but it doesn't become bitter if it sends up a flower stalk. There are green, white, and red selections; of these, red orach is the most common and makes a spectacular border plant. Sow seeds outside once the soil is warm, 1–2 inches (2.5–5cm) apart in rows spaced 12–18 inches (30–45cm) apart; thin later to 6–10 inches (15–25cm) apart. Cut the plants when they reach 12–18 inches (30–45cm) high.

• 'Rhubarb Chard' is a type of Swiss chard with bright red stems and leaf veins (70 days).
• 'Space' is a smooth-leaf spinach suitable for salads or for cooking (40 days).
• 'Tyee' is a spinach with crinkled leaves that is better for cooking (45 days).

Swiss chard may have attractive red stems.

Edible Flowers

A splash of color and flavor

You can add color and interest to your salads and other dishes by scattering in a few edible flower petals, but choose ones that add flavor and texture, too.

When to sow: Spring.

How to sow: Sow annual flowers directly. Simply scratch a line in the soil; scatter the seeds thinly; then cover with soil. You can use them as edging to flower beds or interplant them among rows of vegetables. Sow them in short rows or patterns so you can distinguish them from weed seeds.

Care: Annual flowers are often tough and will thrive on any irrigation or fertilizer aimed at adjacent vegetables. If you let some flowers go to seed, most will spread around the garden. Transplant them if they start to stray too far.

Harvesting: Early morning, once the dew has dried. You don't need to wash them, but make sure you check for insects. The central disk of the flowers can be bitter, so just use the petals.

Choose blossoms such as these nasturtiums, which are edible.

Recommended types:
• Borage has blue cucumber-flavored flowers that are good in salads or floated in summer drinks.
• Calendula is the original marigold and has bright orange, slightly nutty petals.
• Nasturtium has flowers with a distinct peppery taste and comes in a huge range of bright colors.
• Pinks (dianthus) have sweet-tasting petals with a hint of clove.
• Viola provides delicate little flowers that come in a rainbow of colors but add little flavor.

Other Salad Greens

Winter greens

Several other greens are grown to add to salads, and the hardier types, such as corn salad (also known as "lamb's lettuce" or "mâche"), miner's lettuce (or "claytonia"), and upland cress, are good alternatives to lettuce.

When to sow: Late fall to crop through winter.

How to sow: Sow directly into the ground ½ inch (1.3cm) deep in rows 6 inches (15cm) apart. Thin in stages to maintain plants at 6-inch (15cm) intervals. You can use the thinnings in salads.

Care: All of these crops can withstand several degrees of frost, but if it gets really cold, cover them with hot caps. In mild spells, slugs may need removing. Miner's lettuce, which is a native plant, may self-seed readily.

Harvesting: Pick individual leaves, or cut whole plants as required for winter salads. Rinse thoroughly to remove dirt. Corn salad has a mild flavor; miner's lettuce has round, succulent but bland leaves; and upland cress has a peppery flavor reminiscent of watercress.

Corn salad leaves are ideal in a mixture.

Fava Bean

A hardy bean for an early start and a long, warm growing season

Most fava beans, which are also known as "broad beans," are much hardier than bush beans and are worth considering if you want to get an early crop. There are two main types of fava bean: long pods, which are the hardiest and can be sown in fall; and short pods, which are best sown in spring. However, some people can have a serious reaction to fava beans. If you are of African, Mediterranean, or Southeast Asian descent, make sure you consume only fava beans that have been cooked.

Fava Bean

Allow 6 inches (15cm) between plants if they are growing in normal rows.

When to sow: Early spring, or in areas with mild winters, sow in late fall and let them overwinter.

How to sow: Choose a sunny location. Germination will take place within two weeks at 50°F (10°C) in temperature. Sow the large seeds 1–2 inches (2.5–5cm) deep and about 6 inches (15cm) apart.

String or twine provide support for taller plants.

Care: Dwarf types do not need support, but taller plants do. Use posts and string around blocks or along rows to keep plants upright. Mulch to keep down weeds. When the plants are in full flower, pinch off the growing tip to encourage pod formation. In dry weather, water well once a week after flowers fade.

Feel the pod to check whether or not the beans are fully formed.

Harvesting: The first young pods should start to form in early summer. You can pick these and eat them as whole immature pods. If you let the pods reach full size, wait until the beans inside are fully formed. Remove the pods by pulling sharply downward or by cutting them, or you may damage or uproot the plant. The beans should be plump and soft before picking. The scar where the bean joins the pod should be green or white, not discolored. Older beans have a tougher skin, which can be removed after cooking if you prefer. You can blanch and freeze surplus beans. You can also pinch off young edible tips for salads and cook the leaves as you would spinach.

Recommended cultivars:
Long pods, as the name suggests, have long pods with up to eight beans. Short pods have fewer beans.
• 'Express' is a good long-pod type (50–60 days).
• 'Imperial Green Longpod' is another good long-pod type (60–70 days).
• 'The Sutton' produces a good yield of white beans with a good flavor (84 days).
• 'Windsor' has short pods with four round beans; it is better for spring sowing (75 days).

SMART TIP

Pretty enough for a flower bed
The masses of white flowers, each with a black blotch on a petal, make these plants attractive enough for the flower bed. Position them among the other flowers, allowing 18 inches (45cm) a plant. The flowers will also attract beneficial insects.

Bush Bean

Low-growing, undemanding plants

As crops, bush beans need little or no support and provide most of their own fertilizer. You can eat the pods green, wait for the beans in the pods to fill out and eat them, or dry and store the beans for winter use.

When to sow: To ensure a regular supply of green beans, you can make several sowings, starting from early spring in mild areas and continuing until fall. Bush beans are sensitive to frost; wait until after the last frost before sowing outdoors.

A surplus of green beans is ideal for freezing; blanch them in boiling water first.

How to sow: The seeds germinate best when the soil temperature exceeds 55°F (13°C). In cold areas, you can have an earlier crop of beans by sowing them under a floating row cover. Because seed quality will deteriorate quickly, sow only fresh seeds for the best results. Aim to sow the seeds every 3 inches (7.5cm) in rows about 2 feet (60cm) apart. You will need to thin them to 5–6 inches (12.5–15cm) apart. You can also grow bush beans in blocks, with 6 inches (15cm) between plants each way.

Recommended types and cultivars:

• Filet types produce a lot of long, thin beans with a round profile. Pick them often before they reach 4 inches (10cm). Good cultivars include 'Triomphe de Farcy' (48 days) and 'Maxibel' (50 days).
• Purple types produce round, bright purple beans that turn dark green when cooked. 'Royal Burgundy' (60 days) and 'Purple Teepee' (75 days), which holds its pods above the plant, are good cultivars.
• Round-pod types have long, plump pods growing up to 6 inches (15cm) long. Reliable cultivars include 'Blue Lake' (45–50 days), 'Contender' (45–50 days), and 'Tendercrop' (56 days).
• Shelling beans can be produced from any of the larger seeded green types. Good cultivars include 'Borlotti'— do not confuse this with the pole types of the same name— (70 days) and 'Vermont Cranberry' (65 days).
• Waxpods have crisp, round yellow pods (waxy is a misnomer). Cultivars include 'Pencil Pod Wax' (52–60 days).

The beans in these pods are immature, so they are ideal for eating as fresh green beans.

Most bush beans grown in blocks will not require staking.

Care: Bush beans don't require much fertilizer. When the flowers start to appear, make sure the plants never run short of water. A good, thorough soaking once a week will be better than frequent light watering, because the water will penetrate deeper into the soil. Cover with a floating row cover when the temperature starts to drop in fall and there is a threat of frost. Grown in blocks, bush beans should be self-supporting, although taller types in exposed gardens may need support.

Harvesting: Pick green beans for eating fresh regularly, twice a week. If you let the beans in the pods mature, flowering will stop. Pick beans when they are a few inches long to full size, depending on the type. Pick by snapping each bean off using your finger and thumb to avoid uprooting the whole plant. To enjoy the beans at their best, eat straight after picking, cooking lightly.

'Borlotti' is a large cultivar that is ideal for shelling.

Pole Bean

Attractive plants with maximum yields

These beans require more work to grow than bush beans, but because pole beans climb, they make better use of limited garden space. Each plant produces a huge crop of beans over a much longer period.

New shoots will cling to supports as the plant grows.

When to sow: After the last spring frost. The soil temperature should be at least 65–70°F (18–21°C). Choose the cultivar that is right for your climate. Some types do well in cool conditions. In areas with long, hot summers, heat tolerance and disease resistance are important.

Yellow types have flat pods.

How to sow: These beans are always grown using supports. Push two or three beans about 1 inch (2.5cm) deep into the soil near the bottom of each support. Pole beans can easily reach 7 or 8 feet (2.1 or 2.4m) tall in a season and need a structure to climb. You can either work plenty of organic matter into the soil before sowing the seeds or mulch the surface once the plants are established to help retain moisture.

Care: Watering is important for seeds forming inside the pods. When flowers start to form, make sure the plants never run out of moisture—a thorough weekly soaking is more effective than more frequent, but lighter, watering. When the lead shoots of the plants reach the top of the supports, make sure you nip them—this will encourage side shoots to form lower down and give a greater yield.

Bean supports: Use tepee poles. (See "Supporting Beans," below left.) Pole beans can also grow up chain-link or timber fences, trellises, or arches.

Harvesting: If picked regularly—at least twice a week—the plants will produce a crop all summer. Smaller beans are more tender; larger beans have a stronger flavor. Most pole beans can be left to dry and harvested as shelling beans or dried for winter storage.

Supporting Beans

Tepee poles should be at least 8 feet (2.4m) tall. Set them in a circle at least 3 feet (90 cm) across and spaced 12–18 inches (30–45cm) apart. Push the poles well into the ground, and tie the tops firmly. In windy areas, create double rows of poles 2–3 feet (60–90cm) apart, tied and braced with horizontals where they cross at the top. Vertical supports should be 6–8 inches (15–20cm) apart.

Recommended types and cultivars:
• Flat-pod types have wide, flat green pods with visible beans. Try 'Kentucky Wonder' (65 days) and 'Romano' (70 days).
• Purple-pod beans are pretty. Try 'Blauhilde' (64 days) and 'Purple King' (75 days).
• Round-pod types have long, plump pods. Beans are not visible until pods themselves are too mature to eat. Try 'Blue-Lake' (60 days) and 'Fortex' (60 days).
• Shelling beans are produced from the large bean types. Try 'Borlotto Firetongue' (70–80 days).
• Yellow pod types make unusual ornamental plants. Try 'Marvel of Venice' (75 days) and 'Goldfield' (60–70 days).

Pea

Pea

Homegrown pods of sweetness

Frozen peas are so ubiquitous that it is easy to forget the simple pleasure of shelling pea pods and eating fresh, sweet peas straight from the vegetable garden. If you find shelling peas too labor intensive, you can try snow peas or snap peas instead; you eat the pods whole so there's less work—and less waste, too.

When to sow: Peas are hardy plants, so they are a useful early crop. In cold areas, if there's a chance of frost, start them under floating row covers. In cool areas, you can make several sowings through the spring and summer for a succession of fresh peas. However, in hot areas they will suffer in the heat, so confine yourself to early spring and fall crops. In areas with mild winters, a sowing in late fall should survive over the winter for an extra-early crop the following spring. As long as the plants are about 6 inches (15cm) high, they should be able to survive the occasional spell of frost.

How to sow: Peas are usually sown directly into furrows about 6 inches (15cm) wide and 1 inch (2.5cm) deep. Scatter the seeds so that they fall roughly 2 inches (5cm) apart each way. Or sow double rows with seeds 2 inches (5cm) apart. Allow

Once you see flowers beginning to form, you can water the plants.

2 feet (60cm) between the double rows for access. If the soil is dry, water the bottom of the furrow very well before sowing. Dwarf types can also be sown broadcast in blocks. Peas do not like soil that is both cold and wet, so if your soil is very wet, sow them into a raised bed, or on a south-facing slope, where the soil will have the most sun exposure to help reduce excessive moisture.

Using twiggy branches for pea support is a traditional method.

Care: Peas require no fertilizer, but you should work plenty of organic matter into the soil to help retain moisture around the roots. Dwarf types are more or less self supporting. However, tall plants will definitely need supports, and mid-height types can be kept under control by running strings on either side of the rows between 4-foot (1.2m) stakes. Old-fashioned climbing types can be trained like pole beans on tepees, plastic mesh, or fences. You may need to tie stray shoots occasionally.

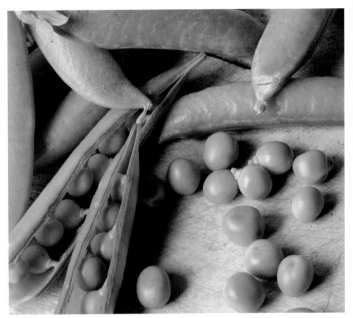

Pea

Flat pods with undeveloped peas indicate that these are snow peas. Both the peas and the pods are eaten and are ideal in stir-fry dishes and salads.

The pods protecting shelling peas are not eaten—only the sweet, tender peas inside them are. If you can't eat them right away, keep them in their pods until the last minute.

Do not water peas until the first flowers begin to form. As the pods start to swell, regular watering in dry spells should increase the yield. Spray peas weekly with a solution of baking soda to help control powdery mildew.

Harvesting: Pick pods regularly to encourage more flowering and more pods to form. Nip off the pods using your index finger and thumb to avoid uprooting the plant. Shelling peas should reach full size, usually 4–5 inches (10–12.5cm). Check that the peas inside are full size and still sweet; they turn starchy with age. Pick snow peas as soon as the pods reach about 2 inches (5cm) up to their full size.

Recommended types and cultivars:

• Shelling peas have plump pods and thin walls. Harvest them when the peas have reached full size but are still sweet. Good cultivars include 'Green Arrow' (70 days), 'Little Marvel' (65 days), and 'Maestro' (60 days), which are all vine types.

• Snap peas have thick, fleshy pods. Pick them before the peas inside develop. They are sweet and crunchy when cooked or eaten raw. 'Sugar Snap' is a reliable older cultivar that grows up to 6 feet (1.8m) tall (68 days). Good modern cultivars include 'Cascadia' (3 feet/90cm; 60 days) and the compact 'Sugar Ann' (55 days) and 'Sugar Bon' (56 days).

• Snow peas have flat pods and are picked before the peas inside develop. 'Oregon Sugar Pod II' grows to about 30 inches (75cm) and does not usually need support (68 days). 'Mammoth Melting Snow', an heirloom type, grows to 5 feet (1.5m) tall (75 days).

Pick snap peas young and eat as snow peas, or harvest with slightly more mature ones when they reach full size. If left too long, the snap peas will be stringy.

SMART TIP

Aphids

Several viruses attack pea plants and cause various symptoms, including yellowing, mottling, and distortion of the leaves. Most are spread by aphids, so try to prevent these from attacking by spraying with insecticidal soap or covering the crops with floating row covers. To remove aphids from the plants, you can try spraying them off using a strong jet of water.

Sweet Corn

Freshly picked for the sweetest flavor

If you like corn on the cob, you will really appreciate it straight off the plant and into the pot. With today's many cultivars from which to choose, even in a short growing season, you will still be able to grow sweet corn. Choose cultivars that are suitable for your area. If you want corn for popcorn, make sure you choose a type that has been specifically developed for that use.

If you sow two seeds together, leave only the strongest plant standing.

When to sow: Wait until all danger of frost is past and the soil is reasonably warm—at least 55°F (13°C)—before sowing corn. It needs to have at least 70–100 days of warm weather from seed to harvest. In short-season areas, choose an early cultivar. Plant your last crop 3 months before the first fall frost date.

How to sow: Grow at least 12 or 16 plants, sowing in a block instead of in rows—for example, three or four rows of four plants each—to ensure good pollination. Space plants 14 inches (35cm) apart each way. Sow seeds in the ground 1–1½ inches (2.5–4cm) deep. Either space seeds 6 inches (15cm) apart and thin out later, or better still, sow two seeds at each position and nip out the weaker one later. In areas with a cold spring and a short season, start seeds in pots where you can maintain a temperature of at least 59°F (15°C). Gradually acclimatize the plants to life outside before planting them outdoors.

Grow corn close together in blocks to help ensure pollination.

Care: Sweet corn needs a position in full sun but with shelter from winds. The soil should be deep, and raised beds will help to warm the soil in spring. Work an inch or so of organic matter into the soil before you plant, and then apply a balanced fertilizer. If the soil is moist at planting time, the

Popcorn

One type of corn has hard kernals that "pop" when heated rapidly—of course, this is popcorn. You can grow popcorn exactly as you do sweet corn. The major difference is that you leave the ears until the stalks turn brown. Cure the ears in a warm, dry place for up to five weeks. Test the kernels at weekly intervals by stripping some from an ear and trying to pop them. When this is successful, strip the remaining kernels and store them in sealed jars somewhere cool.

plants should not need regular watering. To prevent birds from snatching a newly emerging seedling, protect freshly sown seeds with a floating row cover. Corn plants produce offshoots, or tillers, around the base. Although these are unlikely to produce ears, leave them to help feed the main plant. Sweet corn is pollinated by the wind. Each silk sticking out of the developing cob is attached to a female flower, and all need to be pollinated to produce a perfectly filled cob. Planting in blocks instead of rows helps ensure that pollen from the male flowers (the spiky tassels at the top of each plant) falls on the silks lower down. Choose a still day and tap each plant gently when the flowers are fully developed—you'll see clouds of released pollen.

Harvesting: The cobs should be ready to harvest when the silks turn brown and start to dry, about 20 days after the silks first appear. To check, carefully peel back the leaves covering the ear and push a thumbnail into a kernel. If the juice is watery, it's not ready, and if it's starchy, it may be too old. However, milky juice is just right, so pick and eat the corn right away. Be careful to avoid damaging the plant when you pick the corn. Pull the ear downward to snap it off the stalk.

Brown, dried silks are a sign this cob is ready to be picked.

The spiky tassles of the male flowers appear on top of the plants.

Sweet Corn

Recommended types and cultivars:

• Ordinary types, which include heirlooms, are easier to grow and more tolerant of cold summers. Good cultivars include 'Golden Bantam' with yellow kernels (75 days), 'How Sweet It Is' with white kernels (87 days), and 'Silver Queen' with white kernels (92 days).

• Sugar-enhanced types are slightly harder to grow, have more sugar to start, and lose it less quickly. Cultivars include 'Kandy Korn' with yellow kernels (84 days), 'Quickie', which are small plants with bicolored kernels (65 days), and 'Sugar Buns' with yellow kernels (72 days).

• Supersweets are the sweetest types and retain their sugar longer. They are harder to germinate, need ideal growing conditions, and you must isolate them from other types to prevent cross-pollination. Cultivars include 'Early Sunglow' with yellow kernels (63 days), 'Northern Xtra Sweet' with yellow kernels (72 days), and—a good choice for northern gardens—'Indian Summer' with multicolored kernels reminiscent of heirloom Indian corn.

• Extra-tender types are the latest development; these are exceptionally sweet and have such thin skins you can eat them raw straight off the plant. 'Xtra Tender and Sweet' is a good cultivar with yellow kernels.

• Popcorn cultivars are available in a range of colors, including red and blue. Try 'Strawberry' with its small decorative reddish ears. Most need at least 100 frost-free days to mature.

Garlic / Shallot

Garlic

A distinctive, flavorsome bulb

Hardneck garlic produces a false flower shoot and large, full-flavored bulbs. Hardnecks are a good choice for cold areas, but the bulbs don't store well. Softneck types have several layers of small cloves that store well.

When to sow: Garlic plants need a period of cold to start bulb formation, so plant in fall and by spring the plants will be thriving. In very cold regions, plant as soon as you can work the soil in early spring.

How to sow: Start with certified disease-free bulbs from a reputable supplier. Break the bulbs apart and plant the individual cloves. Push them gently into the soil so the pointed tops are just covered. Space the cloves 6 inches (15cm) apart in rows about 12 inches (30cm) apart.

Care: Garlic requires little attention, apart from keeping weeds down. Water in dry spells when the leaves are growing. When the tops start to dry, excavate around the base to reveal the bulbs and expose them to the sun.

Harvesting: When the tops have died off completely, lift the bulbs carefully with a fork and let them bake in the late summer sun for as long as possible. Keep them dry, if necessary, by completing the drying process in a greenhouse or on a sunny windowsill. When completely dry, braid the remains of the tops and hang them in a cool, dry, airy place.

SMART TIP

Tall stiff shoots
Softneck types shouldn't produce a flower stem, but they may do so if there is an interruption to growth. Hardneck garlic will produce a false flower shoot. Cut this while it is soft and green to use in cooking. A ring of cloves will form around the bottom of this stalk.

Shallot

A sweet "multiplier" onion

A planted shallot set or small bulb will multiply into a bunch of a dozen or so shallots during the season.

When to sow: In the North, wait until the soil is workable two to four weeks before the last spring frost date and add general-purpose fertilizer. In the South, plant in fall.

How to sow: You can grow shallots from seeds, but the easiest way to start them is with sets. Simply push each set into the ground until the tip just disappears. Space them about 6 inches (15cm) apart in rows 12 inches (30cm) apart. Sets are usually sold as red or gray, but you may come across named cultivars, such as 'Pikant'.

Care: Keep weeds down with mulch or by hand weeding. Shallots do not need watering unless it is very dry. In this case, a thorough soaking every week or two will increase the size of the bulbs.

Harvesting: When the tops have dried and fallen off and the skins on the bulbs have started to set, lift the clumps with a fork. Let them bake in the sun. In wet weather, bring them indoors to cure. Well-ripened shallots should store well through winter. Keep them somewhere cool and dry; check occasionally for rot. Shallots are smaller and harder to prepare than onions, but they have a sweeter taste and are prized by chefs.

Leek

A mild onion substitute

Leeks have a mild flavor. The white base of the stem is particularly good.

When to sow: In mild areas, you can sow directly into the ground eight weeks before the last spring frost date. Elsewhere, start them in seed-starting trays in early spring.

How to sow: Sow directly in the ground thinly in a furrow ½ inch (1.3cm) deep, or in wide trenches the width of a hoe, aiming for a seed every ½ inch (1.3cm). In trays, aim for the same density. When seedlings straighten and resemble grass, you can tease them apart and replant them individually in divided trays.

Care: When the seedlings are about the thickness of a pencil, they are ready to be transplanted to their final position. Prepare the site by loosening the soil with a fork. Work in a general-purpose fertilizer. Create a trench 4 inches (10cm) wide and deep with a hoe. This will make hilling to blanch the stem bases easier. For plants raised in a seedbed, water to loosen the soil, and then lift and

The white bases are exposed when the outer leaves are removed. Trim off excess green leaf tops.

Use scissors to trim the roots of transplants.

separate them. Trim the roots, as shown above, and some leaves to make transplanting easier. Plant the leeks in the bottom of the trench, using a dibble or trowel, so that just the tips of the leaves are visible. Space the plants about 6 inches (15cm) apart for medium-size leeks. Don't fill the hole, but water the bottom of the trench well to settle the plants. As the plants grow, gradually fill in the trench. You can increase the blanched portions by drawing soil up against the bottom of the plants. Leeks prefer moist soil.

Pests: Guard against slugs and snails.

Harvesting: You can harvest leeks at any stage. When they reach pencil thickness, they are a good, mild substitute for scallions in recipes. To harvest mature leeks, use a garden fork to carefully lever them out of the ground without damaging them. Leeks can be left in the ground until needed. In cold areas, draw straw up against the stems to protect the plants.

Recommended cultivars:
• 'American Flag' is a highly popular fall and winter cultivar (140 days).
• 'King Richard', an early maturing cultivar, can be used as baby leeks or left until it reaches full size (75 days).
• 'Lincoln' is another early maturing type that can be used as baby leeks or left until it reaches full size (50 days).
• 'Pandora' is a modern cultivar good for fall harvest (90 days).

SMART TIP

Red-brown spots on foliage
Leek rust is a fungal disease. Although the leaves are affected, the white base of the plant is still edible. Destroy severely affected plants (making sure they don't end up in your compost pile), and follow a crop rotation to minimize the effects of rust.

Onion

Onion

A pungent bulb available in a variety of sizes and colors

One sowing should provide fresh onions all summer and enough to dry and store for winter, too. Onions are easy to grow from seeds, but you can save time and effort by buying onion sets or started plants.

When to sow: Sow either directly into the ground in spring when the soil temperature reaches 50°F (10°C), or start them in seed-starting trays eight weeks before the last frost date.

How to sow: To sow outdoors, remove all weeds, and rake the soil to create a seedbed. Make seed furrows ½ inch (1.3cm) deep and 6 inches (15cm) apart. Sow thinly, aiming for a couple of seeds per inch. Thin them out later to leave a seedling every 1–2 inches (2.5–5cm). (You can eat these thinnings as you would scallions.) To start seeds in cold areas, grow under cover in trays. Fill a divided seed tray with seed-starting mix and sow a couple of seeds per cell. Cover it with ½ inch (1.3cm) of mix and keep it in a warm, sheltered spot. Transplant outdoors in spring, when the soil temperature reaches 40°F (5°C), about 1½ inches (3.75cm) deep.

Care: Onions are shallow-rooting plants, so they do best in fertile, moisture-retentive soil. They do not need much fertilizer—a little balanced fertilizer is enough. Keep weeds down by hoeing carefully between the rows, being careful not to nick the bulbs or disturb the roots. Hand weed as necessary within the rows.

Harvesting: You can start to pull up fresh onions as soon as the bulbs are large enough. Allow the bulk of the crop to fully mature. When the tops start to dry and fall over, the bulbs will not grow anymore. Carefully lift

A trouble-free crop, you can grow a lot of onions in a small garden.

Yellow onions often have a thicker skin than other types, making them less prone to infection and insects. They are good all-purpose onions.

White onions are available as large bulb types, which are suitable for slicing, and as small bulb types, which are ideal for boiling and pickling.

Red onions have red skin, but the flesh may be white, red, or bicolored. Red Bermuda types are good for serving raw in salads or sandwiches.

them out of the ground with a fork, and lay them raised off the ground to bake in the sun for up to ten days. Let the bulbs dry off and finish curing before storing. Use any damaged bulbs, ones with thick necks, or any that have bolted (produced a flower shoot) first. Store only sound bulbs. The tops should be brown and dry so that you can braid them together.

Recommended types and cultivars:

For spring sowing in the North, choose a long-day onion. In the South, choose short-day types—they need 12-hour days to begin forming bulbs. In mild winter areas, you can also start short-day onions in fall.

- 'Ailsa Craig' is a popular long-day cultivar that produces large brown-skinned onions with a mild flavor (105 days).
- 'Candy', a modern, yellow cultivar, should do well in all states (85 days).
- 'Snow White' is a white-skinned cultivar for all areas (90 days).
- 'Walla Walla Sweet' is a mild sweet-flavored onion, best for northern states (115 days).
- 'Yellow Granex' is a short-day sweet onion, best for southern areas (165 days).

Perfect round onions without thinning
A technique known as multiseeding works well with onions. Sow three to six seeds per cell in a divided seed tray, and let all the seedlings grow. Plant them as a clump; as they grow, they will push apart to create a group of perfect round onions. Space the clumps about 6 inches (15cm) apart.

Bulbs grow just below the soil's surface.

Make sure the onions are completely dry before storing. Keep them in a cool, dry place, and check for rot.

Scallion

An onion for the salad

Scallions, or green onions, are quick and easy crops that you can fit in any spare ground. You can grow them most of the year, and because they take only 10 to 12 weeks from sowing to harvest, it is worth sowing small amounts regularly. Some multiplier onions are perennials that can be divided and harvested every year as scallions.

When to sow: Eight weeks before the last spring frost date, then monthly through spring and summer. In mild areas, make a fall sowing for a winter harvest.

How to sow: Use a hoe to make a furrow 4–6 inches (10–15cm) wide and ½ inch (1.3cm) deep. Scatter the seeds thinly, aiming for a seed every ½ inch (1.3cm); then cover with soil. For clumping types, after the first harvest, replant sections of the clumps to continue your crop. In the following years, the clumps may produce flower stalks and become dormant. However, when temperatures turn cool, they will produce new stems.

Care: Water regularly in dry weather. Keep weeds down by hoeing and hand weeding.

Harvesting: Start pulling scallions as soon as they reach pencil thickness. Pick them as you need them, loosening the soil first with a fork or trowel.

Some scallion types have red skin.

Recommended cultivars:

Scallions are biennials and will produce a small bulb in their first season.
• 'Red Baron' is a modern cultivar with bright red bulbs and green leaves (65 days).
• 'White Lisbon' is a reliable older cultivar (60 days).
• 'Evergreen Hardy White' is a hardy perennial clump-forming cultivar (65 days).
• 'Isikura Improved White' is a single-stemmed cultivar that grows to 12 inches (30cm) tall (50 days).
• 'Tokyo Long White' is a single-stemmed cultivar that grows to about 12 inches (30cm) tall (65 days).

SMART TIP

Growing in containers

Scatter the seeds thinly over the surface of the soil, and cover with a ½-inch (1.3-cm) layer of potting soil. Aim for a seedling every ½–1 inch (1.3–2.5cm) apart each way, but don't worry too much about spacing because the plants will push apart as they grow.

Harvest scallions when they are the thickness of a pencil.

Broccoli

Bright green, sometimes purple-tinted, edible flower clusters

Like cauliflower (page 50), broccoli is unusual because it is the immature flower buds that are eaten—leave one unpicked, and they'll burst into a mass of bright yellow flowers. These heads of flower buds are packed with vitamins and nutrients, which are claimed to help prevent cancer and heart disease.

When to sow: Buying started plants is easier than growing from seeds. Transplant after the last spring frost and again in late spring or early summer for a fall crop.

How to sow: When you are buying started plants, make sure they are healthy and vigorous, are roughly 3 inches (7.5cm) high, and are not rootbound. Broccoli likes a rich, firm soil. Dig in plenty of organic material or a generous dose of plant-starter fertilizer before planting. Set the plants 12 inches (30cm) apart each way to allow for decent-size main heads.

Care: Cover the new transplants with well-secured floating row covers, or be prepared to spray the plants regularly with an organic insecticide. When the main broccoli heads start to form, side-dress the crop with a plant-starter fertilizer to encourage an additional crop, and keep the soil uniformly moist.

The main head has smaller sideshoots flourishing lower down the stem.

Purple sprouting broccoli is hardy and a welcome crop in early spring.

Harvesting: Cut the main head when it reaches full size, usually 3–4 inches (7.5–10cm) across, and the buds are still tight and green. You can leave the broccoli plant in the ground after harvest. Once the main head is cut, sideshoots will start to appear.

These may be smaller, but they are still worth collecting on a regular basis. If you haven't sprayed or covered the crop, check for cabbage worms deep inside the head before preparing it to eat.

Recommended types and cultivars:
• Modern cultivars include 'Green Goliath' (55 days), 'Gypsy' (56 days), and 'Packman' (50 days). They are all quick maturing with large, solid heads.
• Older cultivars, which include 'Green Sprouting' (60–90 days), 'De Cicco' (65 days), and 'Waltham' (79 days), produce over a long period.
• Broccoli alternatives include purple sprouting broccoli, which produces plants with a lot of small, purple heads. It is hardy, and in mild areas you can sow seeds in midsummer for a harvest in early spring.

SMART TIP

Pest control
Fit a root collar around the stem of each plant to stop cabbage root flies from laying their eggs. Place foam rubber or tar paper beneath each transplant so that cabbage maggots will not burrow into the roots. Handpick any caterpillars you see, and crush any eggs.

Brussels Sprouts

Wintertime treat

Brussels sprouts are a useful crop for cold areas, and they are harvested during the fall and winter. After the first frosts, the sprouts hold well on the plants, and the taste becomes sweeter and less harsh. They can also be grown during cool periods in warm regions. If you don't like sprouts because of their bitter taste, maybe you haven't tried homegrown sprouts—these sweeter bundles may change your mind.

When to sow: In the North and cool regions, plant started plants in midsummer. In the South, plant in fall for a spring harvest.

How to sow: Buying started plants is much easier than sowing your own. Don't buy too many—these are large, greedy plants. Plant them 2 feet (60cm) apart each way.

Care: Prepare the soil by digging in plenty of compost or well-rotted manure the previous fall. Don't dig into the soil because the plants need a firm footing. Tread the soil before planting to firm the plants in well. Mulch around the plants during warm weather to keep the roots cool. Feed monthly with a fertilizer. Water in dry spells to keep them growing steadily. Snap off the lower leaves as they become old and brown, leaving just a stump or stem below the developing sprout. A month before the first hard frost is due, cut the leafy topknot—you can cook this like cabbage—if you want the sprouts over a short period. If not, leave the tops until last.

Harvesting: In fall and winter, start picking sprouts from the bottom of the stem upward once they reach about 1 inch (2.5cm) in diameter. They should snap off cleanly. If temperatures below 20°F (-6.5°C) are predicted, cut some plants at ground level; trim off the leaves and excess stem; and store outside the back door.

Recommended cultivars:
• 'Jade Cross', a dwarf and relatively quick-growing cultivar, is good for northern regions and also warm areas with a short cool period (88 days from transplants).

Pick and cook sprouts on the same day for the best flavor.

• 'Oliver' is another dwarf cultivar; however, it requires a slightly longer period to reach maturity from started plants (95 days).
• 'Trafalgar', a tall cultivar at 3 feet (90cm), is suitable for cool areas (up to 130 days).

SMART TIP

Supporting your sprouts
Brussels sprouts are tall, top-heavy plants, susceptible to leaning. This is because their root system is close to the surface. If you plant in firm soil and your yard is sheltered, the plants should be fine. If not, pile up soil around the stems or stake individual plants.

Brussels Sprouts

Cabbage

A versatile vegetable with smooth or crinkly leaves

Cabbage is a cool-weather crop; however, in warm regions, you can still grow it as long as you avoid hot summer temperatures. Choose several cultivars to have a mixture to eat raw or cooked.

When to sow: From early spring to midsummer, depending on your region and the cultivar.

How to sow: You can raise your own seeds indoors for transplanting outside later or buy started cabbage plants. Start the seeds in individual small pots. Plant transplants outdoors to avoid maturing in temperatures above 90°F (32°C). In cool areas, plant in spring, and harvest in summer and fall. In warm areas, plant in early spring, and harvest before hot summer days; plant again in late summer for a fall crop. In hot areas, plant in late summer for a fall harvest and in late winter for a spring harvest. Space early cultivars 12 inches (30cm) apart and late cultivars 18 inches (45cm) apart each way. If you find

conventional cabbages too large, you can try a small-size cultivar at 10 inches (2.5cm) apart.

Use a sharp knife to cut a cabbage head from the stem.

Care: Cabbage plants prefer fertile soil, well supplied with organic matter and nutrients, and constant moisture. Dig in plenty of compost or well-rotted manure, preferably the previous fall. Keep the soil evenly moist by giving it a good soaking once a week during dry spells. Keep insect pests off your cabbage plants by protecting them with a floating row cover. Also, add a high-nitrogen fertilizer three to four weeks after transplanting.

Harvesting: Cut the whole head when it reaches full size. Usually a cabbage head will keep fresh in the ground for a few weeks, or even months in cool weather. Once the shape of a head starts to change and it becomes looser, it is about to bolt—use it immediately. Cut the head to leave a couple of inches of stalk. After a few weeks a baby cabbage will sprout from the stump.

Close spacing between cabbage plants will produce smaller heads.

SMART TIP

Wilting cabbage
Dig up any severely affected plant. If the roots have been mined and nibbled by grubs, cabbage maggots are the culprits. If the roots are swollen and resemble fingers, clubroot disease is the problem. Destroy the affected crop, and plant in a new part of the garden, being careful not to transfer soil, even on your boots. Crop rotation should prevent clubroot, as should adding lime to increase the soil pH to 7.0.

Recommended cultivars:
• Early green cultivars include 'Dynamo', with compact round, green heads that stand well and are resistant to splitting (65 days), and 'Earliana', an early round, green cabbage that can withstand light frost (60 days).
• Late green cultivars include 'Savoy King', with crinkled leaves (80 days from transplants). 'Storage No. 4' has large heads for a fall harvest and storage into spring (80 days).
• Red cultivars include 'Ruby Perfection', which forms dense, medium-size heads that hold and store well (85 days). 'Super Red 80' has medium-size dark red heads resistant to splitting, and stores well, too (78 days).

Cauliflower

A finicky vegetable that's worth the effort

To grow the best cauliflower heads, you need to be dedicated; you have to fight off all kinds of pests, protect the heads from the sun, and provide plenty of food and water. Cauliflower plants are also sensitive to frost, hate hot weather, and produce flower stalks at the least provocation. But if you can pull it off, you'll appreciate the rewards.

When to sow: Plant transplants after the last spring frost date for a summer crop and again in early summer for a fall crop.

How to sow: Buy started plants. Because any interruption to growth can affect the quality of the heads, make sure store-bought started plants are fresh and undamaged and have not been allowed to dry out. Or

The white curds of cauliflower are a delicious treat.

start from seeds indoors; sow them four to five weeks before you plan to transplant them outdoors. Acclimatize transplants well, and being careful to avoid disturbing the roots, bury the plants so the first pair of leaves sit on the soil surface. Cauliflower plants need a rich soil and plenty of water. Work a generous amount of organic matter into the soil, or apply a seed-starter fertilizer before planting. For conventional-size heads, space the plants 18 inches (45cm) apart each way.

Care: Water the transplants well until established. Afterward, don't let the soil become dry. Check that it is moist 6 inches (15cm) below the surface, even if the surface is dry. Apply a fertilizer either as a side-dressing or as a liquid feed when the plants reach full size. Protect the plants with floating row covers buried around the edges; practice crop rotation. Some types are self-blanching and the inner leaves protect the curds. Blanching prevents exposure to the sun, which causes the head to become coarse and yellow. For non-blanching types, check weekly and when the head reaches 2 inches (5cm), if it is exposed, break some of the outer leaves. Fold them over the top of the plant to shade the head.

Harvesting: The ideal time to harvest cauliflower is when the head is full size and the individual buds are still tight and white. If you leave them too long, the buds will become loose and turn into flowers. Cut the stalk below the head, and remove all the outer leaves except a couple of wrapper leaves, which will help protect the curds.

Recommended cultivars:
- White standard cultivars include 'Early White' (52 days), 'Fremont' (62 days), and 'Snow Crown' (50 days).
- Romanesco cauliflowers have unusual green spirelike heads. 'Veronica' is a modern cultivar (85 days).
- Colored cultivars are now available, including 'Cheddar', with pale orange heads (68 days), and 'Graffiti', which has bright purple heads (80 days).

Provide protection to keep insects away from cauliflower.

Chinese Cabbage

Quick-growing exotic cabbage

Chinese cabbage is a quick-growing, space-efficient crop. It suits modern lifestyles and adventurous cooks.

When to sow: It is a cool-weather crop. Sow after midsummer—when the days are shorter—for a fall crop. Modern cultivars can be sown in early spring in cold areas.

How to sow: Start the seeds in pots six weeks before the last frost and plant them outdoors 12–15 inches (30–36cm) apart just before the last frost. Sow fall crops directly in the ground about 90 days before the first fall frost date. Thin in stages to 12–15 inches (30–36cm) apart.

Care: Chinese cabbage really benefits from a well-dug soil with plenty of organic matter. Keep the soil constantly moist (a drip irrigation system is worth considering for this crop). Deter weeds by shallow hoeing to avoid damaging the root system. Give a high-nitrogen liquid fertilizer every other week.

Harvesting: Chinese cabbage can be used at any stage, from seedling to fully formed heads. Cut the whole plant at soil level, and remove the outer leaves until you reach clean ones tightly wrapped around the pale, tender heart, which is the part to eat.

SMART TIP

Pest control
Chinese cabbage is a magnet for the cabbage family pests, such as flea beetles, cabbage caterpillars, and slugs. Protect the crop with floating row covers; use traps or barriers to protect from slugs. Alternatively, you can spray with neem oil soap.

Bok Choy

A cabbage with tender leaves

Bok choy needs a reasonably rich soil and plenty of moisture so that it produces a crop of tender leaves. Any interruption to growth can make it bolt.

When to sow: Bok choy grows best in cool conditions. In cool areas, sow in early spring and again in late summer for a fall crop. In mild regions, sow in late summer to fall for a winter crop.

How to sow: In cold areas, sow seeds in divided seed-starting trays about four weeks before the last frost to plant outdoors after they acclimatize. Sow outdoors in late summer in seed furrows ½ inch (1.3cm) deep and about 8–12 inches (20–30cm) apart. Thin the seedlings in stages to 8–12 inches (20–30cm) apart, depending on the size of the cultivar. Or grow in containers—you can sow them thickly and snip them as baby leaves.

Care: Bok choy grows quickly in rich, moisture-retentive soil. It is also a good candidate for containers filled with

a rich potting mix. Whether growing in pots or the ground, water regularly and feed with a plant-starter fertilizer every other week. These plants also attract the whole range of cabbage family pests; flea beetle can be a real nuisance unless you protect crops with floating row covers.

Harvesting: As with all Asian greens, you can pick bok choy as immature leaves. However, if you want the fleshy white or green stems, let the plants reach full size. You can cut individual leaves from the outside of the plant or pull up the whole plant. A good compromise is to cut the plant an inch (2.5cm) or so above soil level and leave the stump to resprout for a second flush of leaves.

Other Asian Greens

A diverse group of leafy greens

These are all rapid-growing, leafy greans that you can grow in the same way as bok choy. Most, such as the Asian mustards, can be eaten immature as salads, wilted as greens, or added to stir-fries when they are immature. Surprise your guests with these unusual vegetables.

Mibuna and Mizuna: Mibuna has rounded leaves, while mizuna has deeply serrated leaves. Both have a mild mustard flavor, which adds a gentle bite to salads. As the plants reach maturity the leaves become coarse and develop a strong flavor; these are best cooked lightly. For full-grown plants (both take 40 days), thin the seedlings in stages to 12–18 inches (30–45cm) apart. Named cultivars have little to offer compared to unnamed types.

Mizuna, like mibuna, produces leafy, rosette-forming greens.

Mustards are known for their spicy flavors.

Mustards: Mustards are good at spicing up a salad when the leaves are young and tender. They become hotter as they reach maturity, but cooking, by steaming or stir-frying, will mellow them. They are best grown in cool and temperate regions. Sow in early spring and fall. Mustard cultivars include 'Red Giant', with large round red leaves, while 'Miike Giant Purple' has large crinkled leaves (45 days).

Komatsuna: Komatsuna is also known as Japanese mustard spinach, which gives a clue to its flavor—a cabbage somewhere between mustard and spinach. It is tolerant of cold but also fairly resistant to drought, so it can be grown from early spring to fall in all areas. It reaches maturity in 35 days. Sow directly in the soil. For full-grown plants, thin in stages to 12 inches (30cm) apart (35 days).

Komatsuna is a fast-growing crop.

Chinese Broccoli: Chinese broccoli, also known as Chinese kale or gai lan, has glossy blue-green leaves and crunchy flower shoots. Sow in rows 4 inches (10cm) apart. Thin plants in stages to 4–6 inches (10–15cm) apart. Cut the main stem just before the first flower opens and many more shoots will form. It can be grown all year in warm parts but is also suitable for cold areas as a summer crop. 'Green Lance' is a good cultivar (45 days).

Choy Sum: Choy sum, also known as edible rape or yu choy, grows fast in warm areas and can be sown in spring or fall—it may produce flower stalks in hot weather. Pick the first flower shoot at 5–6 inches (12.5–15cm) tall, and more should follow. Both the leaves and flower shoots can be eaten. Use the young leaves and immature flower shoots in stir-fries (45 days).

Hon Tsai Tai: Hon Tsai Tai, or purple-flowered choi sum, is an attractive plant with purple leaves and flower stalks and green leaves. It has a mild mustard flavor and it produces a lot of flower shoots, which you cut before the buds start to open (37 days).

Other Asian Greens

Kale & Collard

A wintertime, nutritious green

Kale thrives in cool areas and is hardy enough to survive hard freezes. Collard has similar growing requirements, but it is more tolerant of heat than kale.

When to sow: Sow or plant in early spring and again in midsummer in cool areas. In hot-summer areas, plant kale only late in the season for a winter crop.

How to sow: Sow seeds thinly into furrows ½–¾ inch (1.3–2cm) deep and 18 inches (45cm) apart. Thin plants to 18 inches (45cm) apart. Or buy transplants.

Care: Provided the soil has plenty of organic matter, kale and collard are easy crops to grow. Make sure the soil doesn't get dry, and apply a little plant-starter fertilizer monthly to encourage rapid growth and tender leaves.

Harvesting: Pick the younger leaves as required and discard the older ones. Rinse to dislodge aphids or other insects. Leave kale to produce flower stalks in the spring. You'll get a flush of tender young leaves and you can use the stalks as you would purple sprouting broccoli.

Kale leaves are best prepared to eat as soon as they are picked.

Recommended cultivars:
• Collard 'Georgia' is a popular cultivar in the South (55 days).
• Kale 'Redbor', a dwarf type, has feathery leaves (55 days).
• Kale 'Black Kale' is an old Italian type. It is worth growing for its striking blue-green leaves (125 days).

Kohlrabi

The eccentric mid-European cabbage relative

You can enjoy kohlrabi for its sweet, crunchy "roots." These are, in fact, swollen stem bases above the ground with leaves attached. This is one of the fast-growing members of the cabbage family, and it is worth planting as a space filler between slower crops. Purple kohlrabi is particularly attractive. Kohlrabi has mild, sweet flavor and can be grated raw in salad or cooked like turnips.

When to sow: Sow seeds for transplants about four weeks before the last spring frost date. Or sow seeds directly into the ground in spring and again four weeks before the first fall frost date. In warm areas, sow until temperatures drop below 40°F (4.5°C).

Care: Kohlrabi grows rapidly. Water regularly during hot weather. Cover with floating row covers to protect from all the pests that attack members of the cabbage family.

Harvesting: Cut kohlrabi just below soil level when the swollen stems reach 1½–2 inches (3–5cm) in diameter. Trim off the lower leaves so that just a tuft of small leaves remains. They have the most flavor just after picking.

Recommended cultivars:
• 'Early White Vienna' is actually pale green, but with white flesh (55 days).
• 'Kolibri' is a newer cultivar with purple skin (50 days).
• 'Purple Danube' is an older cultivar with bright purple skin (65 days).
• 'Purple Vienna' also has bright purple skin (60 days).

Kale & Collard / Kohlrabi

Beet

Beet

Refreshingly sweet, colorful roots

Beets are one of the easiest crops to grow. The large seeds are easy to handle, and provided the soil is moist and rich, they grow rapidly and are attacked by few pests and diseases. They are also one of those easy-going crops that will keep growing until you are ready to harvest.

When to sow: Start sowing seeds in early spring as soon as the soil is workable and there's no chance of a frost. The soil temperature should be at least 50°F (10°C). For a succession of baby beets, make sowings at intervals throughout the summer and into early fall. However, in warm areas stop sowing 60 days before you normally have extreme hot weather. (Beets are a good winter crop in warm areas.)

How to sow: Make seed furrows 1 inch (2.5cm) deep and 12 inches (30cm) apart. Space the seeds 1 inch (2.5cm) apart for baby beets or 2 inches (5cm) apart for large roots. Water the seeds regularly until the seedlings begin to emerge. Beet seeds are not really true seeds but are, in fact, corky fruit containing up to four seeds. That explains why several seedlings come up together however carefully you space them. They will push themselves apart as they grow.

A bulbous beet appears above ground.

Care: Beets are greedy feeders, so be generous with compost when you prepare the bed, or add some plant-starter fertilizer before sowing. Apart from keeping down weeds while they are getting established, beets need little attention, especially if you apply a mulch. Beets shouldn't need watering unless the soil becomes dry.

Harvesting: You can start picking the young leaves to use in salads about four weeks after sowing the seeds, or prepare the older leaves in the same way that you would prepare spinach. Harvest baby beets as soon as they reach 1–1½ inches (2.5–3.5cm) in diameter (these are suitable for pickling). Twist off the foliage, and leave the thin taproot intact—this will help prevent the color from bleeding excessively when they are cooked. Don't peel the roots until after cooking for the same reason.

Recommended types and cultivars

Avoid "monogerm" types, which have been bred to carry a single seed in each cluster. This is an advantage for commercial growers but not for the gardener.

• Baby beets can be harvested from round, red, quick-maturing cultivars, such as 'Red Ace' (53 days), 'Red Cloud' (60 days), or 'Detroit Dark Red' (60 days).

• 'Albina' is a white beet; it does not stain and is sweet and tasty (55 days).

• 'Burpees Golden' has golden skin and flesh. It tastes the same as red types but doesn't stain (55 days).

• 'Chioggia' is an heirloom type with a pink skin and alternate pink-and-white rings when cut in half. The color bleeds when cooked, leaving it a pale pink (54 days).

• 'Cylindrica' is a long-root, red cultivar; grow it if you like sliced beets (60 days).

• 'Forno' is another good choice if you are looking for a long-root beet (55 days).

Carrot

Crunchy and nutritious, harvest them young for the sweetest baby carrots ever

Carrots are a trouble-free backyard crop if soil conditions are right. The soil needs to be light, loose, deeply dug to 12 inches (30cm), and free of stones. The seeds are tiny, so use seed tape or pelleted seeds to make planting easier.

SMART TIP

Carrot rust fly
The grubs of the carrot rust fly are attracted to the carrot smell when you thin or harvest carrots. To prevent them, cover the plants with floating row covers and thin or harvest in the evening when the flies are not active.

Carrot

When to sow: For fresh carrots, choose an "early" type and make several sowings at intervals from very early spring until early fall. For winter-storage carrots, choose a "full-size" type and make one sowing in early summer.

How to sow: Make a seed furrow ½ inch (1.3cm) deep. If the soil is dry, water the furrow and let it drain. Space rows 12 inches (30cm) apart. Scatter the seeds thinly to avoid having to thin out seedlings later. As a guide, aim for a seed every ½ inch (1.3cm).

Care: Keep weeds down until the carrot plants become well-established, either by hoeing carefully between the rows or hand weeding. When the seedlings have rooted well, thin them so there is a plant every 1 inch (2.5cm). Water the row deeply just once a week to keep the soil evenly moist at a good depth—unlike frequent, shallow watering, this will encourage deep rooting.

Harvesting: You can start pulling carrot roots as soon as the tops of the roots reach about ½ inch (1.3cm) across. Either carefully pull up individual larger roots, leaving the rest to grow, or dig up sections of a row together. Use a garden fork to carefully loosen the soil to avoid breaking longer roots.

Recommended types and cultivars:
Early types are ready for harvest in as little as 50 days after seeds are sown, and they are a good choice for growing in containers.
• 'Amsterdam' types will grow rapidly to finger size; 'Minicor' (55 days) is a typical cultivar.
• 'Chantenay' types, such as the cultivar 'Chantenay Red Cored' (70 days), produce short and broad-shouldered roots. These are better for growing in shallow soil.
• 'Nantes' types, such as the cultivars 'Nantes Half-Long' (70 days) and 'Touchon' (65 days), produce slim, blunt-ended roots up to 6 inches (15cm) long.
• 'Round' or 'Paris Market' carrot types are a good choice if your soil is shallow or stony. 'Parmex' (50 days) and 'Thumbelina' (60 days) are typical cultivars.

Full-size carrots are slower growing but produce a higher yield by fall. These include:
• 'Danvers', a type of large, broad-shouldered carrot, of which 'Danvers Half-Long' (75 days) is a typical cultivar.
• 'Imperator' types produce narrow, pointed roots up to 10 inches (25cm) long. Cultivars include 'Canada Gold' (75 days).
• Unusually colored cultivars include 'White Satin', with sweet white roots (65 days); 'Purple Haze', with purple skins but orange flesh (70 days); and 'Rainbow', a mix of white, pale yellow, and pale orange (75 days).

Start harvesting carrots when the tops of the roots reach ½ in. (1.3cm) across, selecting the largest roots first.

Celery

A subtle but distinctive vegetable, raw or cooked

Celery is an essential ingredient for the cook. It is the basis of a well-flavored vegetable stock, and it is good raw in a salad. It thrives in cool, damp conditions and needs a long growing period to produce its tasty, crunchy stems.

When to sow: Sow into pots eight weeks before the last expected spring frost. Plant outdoors when average daytime temperatures exceed 55°F (13°C).

How to sow: Soak the seeds in a compost tea for six hours before sowing. The seeds need light to germinate—sow on the surface of the potting mix and cover very thinly. Keep at 65°F (18°C) until germination occurs; then leave outdoors a little longer each day so they get used to colder temperatures. Prepare the bed by digging in plenty of garden compost or well-rotted organic matter to retain moisture. Space about 9 inches (23cm) apart each way in blocks, not rows.

Care: Mulch around the plants with straw or organic matter to keep the soil cool and retain moisture. Water regularly to keep the soil consistently moist, and cover

Blanch some celery cultivars by placing a collar around the stems.

with floating row covers. Self-blanching cultivars, such as 'Golden Self-Blanching' and 'Tango', mature quickly and are less work than others, which need to be blanched. Feed the plants weekly with a fish emulsion to keep them growing strongly.

Harvesting: You can cut off individual stalks from the outside of the plant as soon as they are large enough for your needs, or wait and dig up the whole plant. Because celery is very sensitive to cold, harvest the plants before the first hard frost in the fall.

Celeriac

The taste of celery, with a hint of nutty flavor

The fleshy root of celeriac is a good alternative to celery, its close relative.

When to sow: Before the last spring frost. In warm areas, start celeriac in summer for a winter crop. Celeriac needs a long season of 110 days or more from sowing, so purchase started plants or raise your own transplants.

How to sow: Sow seeds into small pots before the last spring frost. Cover the seeds lightly—they need light to germinate. Harden off the seedlings gradually, and plant outdoors when 2–3 inches (5–8cm) tall.

Care: Work plenty of organic matter into the soil before planting transplants to help retain moisture. Give plants plenty of room, about 12 inches (30cm) each way. Keep the soil uniformly moist by regularly soaking the soil to a good depth. Keep weeds down with regular hoeing, being careful not to nick the roots with the blade. In hot weather, keep the soil cool and moist by mulching, which will also help to keep the weeds down.

Harvesting: Start to dig roots when 4 or 5 inches (10–13cm) across. You can store the roots by leaving them in the ground until needed. Cover them with straw to protect them from frost. In late fall, before the soil freezes, lift the roots; pull off all the leaves except the innermost tuft to prevent rotting; and store in boxes of barely moist sand.

Celeriac's large, knobby root has a distinctive celery flavor.

Celery / Celeriac

Parsnip

A wintertime treat

Parsnips are slow-growing crops. The white roots really come into their own in winter. Although you can harvest young, tender roots earlier, this is one crop to leave until after the first fall frosts.

When to sow: Sow once in late spring when the soil is warm and moist.

How to sow: Parsnip seeds are attached to a flat membrane and can be blown around. As a precaution, sow several seeds together. Dig and loosen the soil to at least 18 inches (45cm) if you want long, straight roots. Make furrows ½ inch (1.3cm) deep and 12 inches (30cm) apart, and water the bottom if the soil is dry. Sow seeds 1 inch (2.5cm) apart. When the seedlings are 4–6 inches (10–15cm) tall, thin to 4 inches (10cm) apart. Because the seedlings can be slow to appear, an old-timers' trick is to sow radish seeds in the same furrow. These will appear quickly, marking the row.

Care: In the early stages, hoe regularly between the rows to keep weeds down, but be careful to avoid damaging the seedlings. When the seedlings reach a few inches tall, apply a mulch of chopped leaves to suppress weeds and conserve water. Provided the soil is moist before sowing, they should not need additional watering. However, do not let the soil dry out at depth; drought followed by rain will cause the roots to split. Apply a general fertilizer as a side-dressing or spray with compost tea in midsummer.

Use a garden fork to lift parsnips out of the ground.

Keep your parsnips in the ground until the first fall frost.

Harvesting: The flavor improves after a frost. The best way to store the crop is by leaving them in the garden. A thick mulch will extend the harvest in cold regions.

Recommended cultivars:
• 'Andover' is an older cultivar with slender roots (120 days).
• 'Gladiator', a modern cultivar, is resistant to canker (110 days).
• 'Harris Model' is a medium-size cultivar (120 days).
• 'Javelin' is good for baby roots (110 days).

Unusual Roots

All three of the following root crops are grown in the same way as parsnip and can also be left in the garden until needed:
• Hamburg parsley is a type of parsley bred for its parsniplike roots. You can use the leaves, but they are coarser than normal parsley. Roast the roots like those of parsnips (90 days).
• Salsify is a biennial, so it will flower in the second year. It has grasslike leaves, and the roots are long and thin and are said to taste of oyster. You can boil the roots in vegetable stock and roast the larger ones (100 days).
• Scorzonera is a perennial, so if the roots aren't large enough after a year, you can let it grow for a second year. It has wider leaves and long, thin, black-skinned roots. The flesh discolors easily, so scorzonera is best cooked whole and peeled later (120 days).

Salsify has long, thin roots.

Potato

The great staple of the vegetable garden that is so rewarding

Potatoes require plenty of space, but few vegetables will provide you with such a prolific crop at the end of the season. Apart from the late-season types, which can be stored through winter, there are the fast-growing earlies, ready to harvest after only a few months. Later cropping, but also good fresh out of the ground, are the waxy salad and the fingerling types. If you have limited garden space, try growing potatoes in containers.

When to sow: Plant sprouted tubers about three weeks before the last expected spring frost.

How to sow: Potatoes are grown from "seed potatoes"—tubers with "eyes," or buds. You can buy seed potatoes from a garden center or mail-order company. Prepare a trench 6–8 inches (15–20cm) deep and the width of a spade. In light soil, make the trench 12 inches (30cm) deep and fill halfway with compost to help retain moisture. For heavy or poorly drained soil, grow potatoes in raised beds. Space the rows 30 inches (75cm) apart for mid- and late-season crops and 18 inches (45cm) for early-season crops. Plant small seed potatoes under 1½ ounces

The eyes of the seed potatoes will eventually sprout.

(42.5g) whole or cut larger ones into sections, making sure that each section has two or three eyes (buds). Let the cut seed potatoes "cure" in a warm place for a few hours to two days. Plant the cured tubers or pieces about three weeks before the last expected spring frost. Lay the seed tubers at 12-inch (30cm) intervals along the bottom of the trench and fill with soil.

Care: Potatoes will grow perfectly well on flat ground; however, because the tubers form near the surface of the soil, a portion of them are often pushed out of the soil and, if exposed to light, they will turn green. Areas on potatoes that are green are slightly toxic if eaten. Fortunately, the technique of "hilling," or piling up the soil in stages will prevent this. In a few weeks after planting the seed potatoes, shoots should emerge from the soil; protect these from any risk of frost with floating row covers. When the shoots reach 4–5 inches (10–12cm)

tall, start to pile up the soil by drawing it around the bottom of the plants to form hills. Keep doing this as the plants grow until the hills are 12 inches (30cm) high. Water early types regularly throughout their growth. However, do not water late-season types until the flowers start to appear—tubers will be forming underground at this stage and plentiful water will increase the yield.

Harvesting: Early-season types are ready to harvest as soon as the plants start to flower, about 60 days after planting. Mid-season cultivars are normally ready to harvest in about 80 days, and you can harvest them fresh—before the skins begin to become tough—or let them mature. Late-season types are ready for harvesting after about 90 days, usually two weeks after the tops die down, as long as there's no threat of frost. Use a fork to loosen the soil; then remove the tubers with your hands to avoid skewering them with the fork. Choose a dry fall day, and lay out the tubers to dry for a few hours; then spread them out in a cool, dark place for a week to cure and store in paper or burlap sacks in a cool, dark place to use through the winter. When harvesting, reject any damaged tubers for storing; you can use them immediately.

Recommended types and cultivars:

• Early-season cultivars include 'Caribe', which has purple skin and white flesh (70–90 days); 'Red Norland', a very early type with red skin and white flesh (90–100 days); 'Red Pontiac', an all-purpose cultivar with bright red skin and white flesh; and 'Yukon Gold', an early to mid-season cultivar with yellow skin and flesh (70–90 days).

• Mid- and late-season types are numerous. You can try 'Kennebec', a versatile yellow-fleshed cultivar that tastes good and stores well (100–110 days).

• Fingerlings are popular types with long, thin tubers, firm, waxy flesh, and an unsurpassed flavor. 'Peanut Fingerling' has russet skin and firm, yellow, nutty flesh (105–135 days); 'Rose Finn Apple' has long, knobbly, pink tubers with firm, waxy flesh (105–135 days); and 'Russian Banana' is a gourmet cultivar with yellow skins and flesh (105–135 days).

• Unusual cultivars to try include 'All Blue', with blue skin and blue-and-white flesh (110–135 days), and 'All Red', with red skin and pink flesh (70–90 days).

SMART TIP

Growing in containers

You'll need a large container with a capacity of 2 gallons (7.5L), preferably more, filled halfway with a rich potting mix. Bury a sprouted tuber of an early or salad type into the soil. As the tops grow, cover them with layers of potting mix until you reach the top of the container. Water regularly. If you use a rich potting mix, extra feeding will not be necessary. When the tops start to yellow and die, usually after about two months for an early type, you can start harvesting the potatoes. Either empty the pot and harvest the whole crop, or push your hand into the container and feel for tubers the size of an egg or larger, leaving any tiny ones to continue growing.

Dig up all the potatoes at once, or pull them up a few at a time—the choice is yours.

After harvesting, let the potatoes air dry for a few hours.

Hilling the soil will prevent the tubers from turning green. Do this as the plants grow.

Radish

Colorful roots with a zesty flavor

Radishes are so quick and easy to grow that you can get several crops through the year. Grow them in containers, or fit them between other slower-growing vegetables.

When to sow: Sow small amounts every 10 to 14 days from early spring, as soon as the soil can be cultivated, until fall. In hot-summer areas, stop sowing during the summer, but continue sowing through winter.

How to sow: Loosen the soil to make a seedbed, and sow into furrows ½ inch (1.3cm) deep and 6 inches (15cm) apart. As a fill-in crop, sow midway between adjacent longer-term crops. Sow the seeds thinly, and when the seedlings appear, usually in less than a week, thin them to about 1 inch (2.5cm) apart.

Care: Summer radishes should grow quickly and without an interruption to growth, so make sure you keep the soil moist at all times.

Harvesting: Start pulling individual roots when they reach 1 inch (2.5cm) in diameter, leaving the remainder to continue growing. Alternatively, pull up as bunches, and discard the undersize roots.

Harvest radishes when 1–2 in. (2.5–5cm) across.

Recommended types and cultivars:
• Long-Root types include 'French Breakfast', which is a red type with a white tip (25 days), and 'White Icicle,' which is an all-white cultivar (30 days).
• Round Red types include 'Cherry Belle' (23 days) and 'Sparkler' (25 days).

Winter Radish

Large roots, either hot or mild

Also known as daikon or mooli, the winter radish produces large roots.

When to sow: Sow thinly in midsummer so the harvest coincides with the first fall frost.

How to sow: Thin to 6 inches (15cm) apart in rows about 10 inches (25cm) apart.

Care: Apart from the occasional weeding and watering, they require little attention.

Harvesting: You can pull the roots anytime and use them fresh as summer radishes. They will store better if you leave them to develop to their full size and color. Leave in the garden until needed, but dig up before the soil freezes. Hot types have a better flavor when cooked. Milder types are best raw or grated into salads.

Recommended cultivars:
• 'April Cross' is a long, pointed, all-white cultivar with a mild flavor (65 days).

• 'Black Spanish Round' is a hot-flavored cultivar with black skin and white flesh (60 days).
• 'Summer Cross' is a long, pointed cultivar with a mild flavor (45 days).

The winter radish is also known as daikon radish.

Sweet Potato

A hot-weather producer of sweet roots

Sweet potatoes will thrive in hot weather, but because the slightest frost will kill the vines, it is risky to attempt to grow them in colder areas. They are normally grown in the southern states, where they should get the minimum 100 warm days and nights that they need. However, if you pick a quick-yielding cultivar, they are still well worth a try in other areas. Nutrient-packed sweet potatoes are often confused with yams, but yams are from Africa and Asia, while sweet potatoes are an American native.

When to sow: Sweet potatoes are not grown from seeds but are grown from rooted cuttings known as "slips." Buy certified disease-free slips from a nursery or mail-order supplier. Plant in spring after there is no risk of frost.

How to sow: Plant the slips deeply, so the first leaves are level with the ground. For the best results, make sure you plant the slips in loose, stone-free soil with little or no fertilizer. Mound the soil until it's about 8 inches (20cm) high, with 3 feet (90cm) between rows, and plant the slips about 18 inches (45cm) apart. In cooler parts, grow sweet potatoes in raised beds—the soil temperature will be warmer.

Use garden wire or twine to help keep vines off the ground.

Care: Cover with floating row covers early and late in the season to protect the crop from frost and prolong the season. Once established, sweet potatoes do not need to be fed or watered. As the temperature increases, the vines will grow rampantly. You should lift the vines off the ground to prevent them from rooting as they grow. This concentrates the plants' energy back to the initial roots, where the tubers will form.

Harvesting: Let the plants die down; the first frost will kill the tops. Dig up the tubers, carefully easing them up with a garden fork. Cure them by setting them in the sun for a day; then in a warm, humid place for 10 to 14 days. Wrap each tuber in newspaper, or place the tubers on racks, and keep in a cool, dry place for up to five months.

Recommended cultivars:
• 'Beauregard' is a high-yielding cultivar with red skin and light orange flesh; it is suitable for most areas with long growing seasons (105 days).
• 'Georgia Jet' also has red skin and orange flesh; this cultivar is suitable for cooler areas (90 days).
• 'Vardaman' has a golden skin, orange flesh, and shorter vines; it is a good choice for smaller gardens or containers (110 days).

When digging up the tubers, avoid piercing the skin with the garden fork.

Turnip

Turnips will produce usable roots, such as these, only eight weeks after sowing.

Turnip

White roots and succulent greens

Turnips are so quick-growing they make a useful fill-in crop among the more slow-growing members of the cabbage family. Apart from the sweet, slightly hot-flavored roots, they provide valuable edible greens in spring and fall.

When to sow: A few weeks before the last frost date. Make several sowings through the season, but in warm regions, stop sowing in the hottest part of the year.

How to sow: Turnips benefit from a moist, fertile soil, so work in an inch (2.5cm) of well-rotted organic matter or a generous amount of a plant-starter fertilizer before sowing. Make seed furrows ¾ inch (2cm) deep and 6 inches (15cm) apart. Sow thinly and water well. Thin the seedlings to 4 inches (10cm) for roots or 1½ inches (3.75cm) for turnip leaves.

Care: Water them regularly during dry spells. Give a thorough soaking once a week instead of just wetting the surface. Keep weeds down by applying a mulch, which will also help retain moisture. Otherwise, regularly hoe

between the rows, but avoid damaging the roots with the blade. Like their leafy relative the cabbage, turnips are susceptible to insect pests—flea beetle, cabbage root maggots, and cabbage caterpillars. Cover with floating row covers before the seedlings appear to keep all these pests away. Cabbage root maggots tunnel into the roots early in the season, so you can also avoid these by sowing turnip seeds in late spring or midsummer.

Harvesting: Lift turnips as baby roots when they reach 2 inches (5cm), or let them grow to 4 inches (10cm) across. Trim off the leaves. Cut greens for cooking when plants are 6 inches (15cm) high. Leave a stump 1 inch (2.5cm) high, and more leaves will grow.

Recommended cultivars:
• 'Hakurei' is very fast, has flattened white roots, and is a good choice for greens (38 days).
• 'Purple Top White' is a standard bicolored cultivar (55 days).
• 'Tokyo Cross' is a fast-growing all-white globe, good for baby roots (40 days).

Rutabaga

A cool-weather crop

A winter staple, rutabaga is good as a hearty roasted vegetable or in stews.

When to sow: Midsummer for a fall harvest. Rutabaga takes as long as four months to grow, so it will be in the garden for a long time.

How to sow: Sow thinly into furrows 1 inch (2.5cm) deep and 15 inches (38cm) apart. Thin the seedlings in stages to 9 inches (23cm) apart.

Care: Rutabaga needs little attention, apart from some occasional weeding and watering to prevent the soil from drying out completely deep down.

Recommended cultivar:
• 'American Purple Top' is a standard cultivar with a purple top and yellow flesh (100 days).

Leave in the ground until needed or a hard freeze is due.

Rutabaga / Florence Fennel

Florence Fennel

A bulb with a mild licorice flavor

Though not a root, Florence fennel forms a swollen stem base that is eaten as a vegetable.

When to sow: In areas with a short summer, start seeds in small pots in a warm place. In warm areas, you can sow seeds directly in spring or summer. In the hottest areas, sow in midsummer for a fall harvest.

How to sow: Florence fennel seeds can be difficult to find. Try looking under "finocchio" in seed catalogs. Florence fennel needs a cool but frost-free period of about 100 days. Very hot or cold weather or lack of water will make it send up flower shoots or produce tough, stringy bulbs. Space plants about 12 inches (30cm) apart. If you have started the seeds in small pots, bring the seedlings outside a little longer each day until they are acclimatized to the outdoors. Plant outside when there's no chance of a late frost.

Care: Keep seeds and seedlings moist. Water regularly to keep the soil moist and ensure uninterrupted growth. An occasional application of fish emulsion in the summer will help, too.

Harvesting: You can harvest the bulbs when they are 3–5 inches (7.5–12.5cm) across. Cut the aboveground bulb from its roots; trim off the leaf stalks; and use the bulbs immediately for the best flavor.

The swollen stem bases are suitable for eating.

Pepper & Chili

Pepper & Chili

From sweet and mild to fiery hot

Bell peppers and hot chilies are easy plants to grow from seeds; but they are even easier to grow if you buy named started plants from a garden center in late spring. The plants need little care—just a regular supply of water. Most do best with plenty of heat and a long growing season, but there are also cultivars that should succeed in the coldest areas, too.

When to sow: Eight weeks before the last frost date.

How to sow: Peppers are easy to grow from seeds but need plenty of warmth to germinate and are slow to grow to transplanting size. Start off the seeds in individual pots or divided seed-starting trays. The germination temperature should be about 80°F (27°C). Instead of sowing seeds, you can buy young pepper plants in late spring, especially if you want to try a variety of shapes, colors, and levels of heat. Wait until the soil reaches 70°F (21°C) before planting home-raised or store-bought transplants into the garden. Space them about 15 inches (38cm) apart.

When harvesting any type of pepper or chili, use a sharp knife.

Care: Peppers need a lot of warmth, so choose a spot sheltered from wind in full sun. Cover the soil with a black plastic sheet to help warm the soil, retain moisture, and prevent weeds. Peppers need a moderately rich soil, so work a little organic matter into the bed before planting. The soil should be free-draining, too. Cover new transplants with floating row covers to keep them warm and protected from pests. Most cultivars will form compact bushes. If necessary, prune any long shoots to keep the plants neat and encourage branching. Water the plants regularly to keep the soil just moist, but not too wet, about 1 inch (2.5cm) a week. A drip irrigation system is ideal, and it will save on work. Once you have a strong plant and the fruit begins to form, apply a high-potassium fertilizer.

Harvesting: Cut both sweet bell peppers and chilies at any stage. Green bell peppers will be less sweet and green chilies less hot than fully ripe red ones. However, if you pick the fruit while under-ripe, it will prolong the harvest and you'll have more peppers to pick. Fully ripe peppers usually turn red, but if you let them mature and develop seeds, the plant will stop producing fruit.

Recommended cultivars:
Harvest days are from planting out to green fruit; the higher number is for fully ripe fruit. Peppers grow slowly in cold soil, so choose cultivars to suit your climate.
• 'Ace' is an early bell pepper, reliable in short-season areas; it ripens to bright red (60–80 days).
• 'Anaheim' is a mild chili pepper, with long tapered green fruit ripening to red (77 days).
• 'Blushing Beauty' is a big, sweet bell pepper that starts yellow and develops a pink-red blush when mature (72 days).
• 'Californian Wonder' is the standard bell pepper with large, blocky fruit that turns from green to red; ideal for stuffing (75 days).

- 'Carmen', a modern type of banana pepper, is light green to bright red and pointed (60–80 days).
- 'Early Jalapeno' is a mild chili with blunt, dark green fruit 3 inches (7.5cm) long (60–80 days).
- 'Gypsy' is a banana pepper with beautiful, elongated tapered fruit that turns from yellow to orange to red; good for short-season areas (65–85 days).
- 'Holy Mole' is a very mild chili with dark green fruit 7–9 inches long (18–23cm) that ripens to dark brown; good in Mexican cuisine (85 days).
- 'Hungarian Hot Wax' is a large, fairly mild, pointed pepper that ripens through yellow to red (70–95 days).
- 'Mariachi' is a hybrid chili cultivar with mild but very attractive carrot-shaped, yellow and red fruit 4 inches (10cm) long (65 days).
- 'Sweet Banana', another banana pepper, has pointed yellow fruit 6–7 inches (15–18cm) long that ripens to red (72 days).
- 'Sweet Chocolate' is an unusual reddish brown bell pepper, good for short-season areas (65–90 days).
- 'Thai Hot' is a very hot chili with bright red fruit about 3½ inches (9cm) long (75–95 days).

Growing in Containers

Sweet peppers and chilies in particular make neat, bushy container plants. Choose cultivars that are naturally compact, such as 'Baby Belle', or cut back 8-inch (20cm) or longer branches by one-third to encourage bushiness. Using a small container, about 8 inches (20cm) in diameter, will also keep the plant compact, but it will need more frequent watering. Keep the plants well watered—a drip irrigation system will cut down on your work— and feed regularly with a high-potassium fertilizer, such as one used for tomatoes.

Pepper & Chili

Banana peppers, another type of sweet pepper, have long, pointed fruit that grow up to 6 inches (15cm) long; the fruit can be yellow, orange, or red when ripe.

Bell peppers are the familiar squat, square-shape sweet peppers, available in a range of colors, including green, red, yellow, orange, and even purple.

A type of chili, poblano peppers have a hint of heat at a rating of 1,000 to 1,500 heat units on the Scoville scale. (See the glossary on page 93.) At 4 to 6 inches (10–15cm) long, these peppers are good for stuffing.

Habanero peppers need a long hot season to produce 2-inch (5 cm) long, extremely hot fruit—their Scoville rating can top the scale at 200,000 heat units or greater! They ripen from green to gold before they mature to orange.

Eggplant

Eggplant

Beautiful in the garden, delicious on the plate

Unlike many other vegetable plants, eggplant is attractive enough for either a flower border or prominent container planting. Why confine yourself to purple when there are so many interesting colors? Eggplant will grow in most hardy zones, but they are heat-loving plants that can be temperamental in the North. Choose short-season cultivars to grow in these areas.

When to sow: Eight weeks before the last frost date.

How to sow: Start seeds in divided seed-starting trays. Keep them at 80°F (27°C), using a warming mat to provide bottom heat. You can also buy young plants in late spring from a garden center. Wait until the soil reaches 70°F (21°C) before planting transplants. Try not to disturb the rootball and space 24 inches (60cm) apart each way.

Care: Eggplant prefers plenty of heat, so give it a sheltered position, away from wind, in full sun in cooler areas. It also likes a rich but well-drained soil that warms up quickly in spring. Apply a high-potassium fertilizer to keep the plants growing strongly and encourage the crop to grow rather than the leaves.

Harvesting: Cut an eggplant when it reaches about half its full size. It will be sweet and tender, and this will encourage the plant to keep producing more. Choose an eggplant with shiny skin.

Recommended cultivars:
• 'Black Beauty', a classic, large, dark purple eggplant (80 days).
• 'Dusky', a good dark-fruit cultivar suitable for the North (63 days).
• 'Purple Rain' has lighter purple fruit than most, flecked with cream.
• 'Fairy Tale', a modern, less-spiny cultivar, produces bunches of small, elongated fruit up to 4 inches (10cm) long, beautifully striped white and purple; good for containers (65 days).
• 'Ichiban' is an Asian cultivar with purple, elongated fruit (70 days).
• 'Kermit' has small, mottled, round green-and-white fruit, about 2 inches (5cm) across (60 days).
• 'Rosa Bianca', an Italian heirloom with white-and-mauve striped fruit, is best for warm areas (75 days).
• 'Snowy' produces medium-size, pure white, elongated fruit (60 days).

Use upturned pots to keep the fruit off the ground.

SMART TIP

Growing in containers
The eggplant is a great container plant, attractive enough to hold its own with ornamental plants—but with the bonus of tasty fruit, too. In a small container about 12 inches (30cm) in diameter, they make neat bushes that are covered in soft leaves and bright yellow flowers. Choose a modern, less spiny cultivar with plenty of small fruit—'Fairy Tale' is one of the best. Feed eggplant regularly with a tomato fertilizer.

Tomatillo

A tart tomato-like fruit with firm flesh

This vegetable is hardier than its relative the tomato, and is less likely to suffer from pests and diseases. The fruit itself grows inside a brown, papery husk. The similar ground cherry, also known as the cape gooseberry or physalis, is sweeter than the tomatillo.

When to sow: About four weeks before the last frost.

How to sow: Tomatillos and ground cherries are easy to grow from seeds and self-seed readily. First, sow the seeds in individual pots or divided seed-starting trays. Sow directly or plant outdoors 3 feet (90cm) apart when the soil has started to warm up. Grow them in full sun on soil that is not too rich; they require no additional fertilizer.

Care: Water the plants only in very dry spells. You can prune long branches to help keep the plants compact and bushy. Alternatively, grow them inside tomato cages, like tomatoes, to keep them neat. You should treat them as a member of the tomato family when planning a crop-rotation plan to prevent soil diseases.

Harvesting: The fruit is ready to pick when it is completely full and starts to split its husk. It will often start to drop when ready. Any fruit not gathered will produce seedlings next season, so harvest as many fruit as you can. Tomatillos are ripe when they turn yellowish green or purple. Ground cherries will turn golden yellow. Both can be stored—leave them in the husks—for a month or two if spread out and kept in a cool place.

Tomatillos have green, papery husks that change color as they ripen.

Okra

A mild-flavored vegetable with an unusual texture

Okra originated in Africa and needs all the heat it can get. It is a crop that thrives in the warmest parts of the South. However, there are now hybrids that will succeed as a summer crop in the colder North.

When to sow: Okra will not germinate or grow well when the soil temperature is below 70°F (21°C). Wait until the soil is warm enough in mild climates, and sow the seeds directly into the ground. In the North and cool areas, start okra in pots or divided seed-starting trays indoors about three to four weeks before the last frost date.

How to sow: If planting directly, sow the seeds about 3 inches (7.5cm) apart in rows 1½–3 feet (45–90cm) apart. When the seedlings are large enough, thin to 12 inches (30cm) apart. Most cultivars need 50–70 warm days, so sow the seeds at several intervals until about 16 weeks before the first fall frost is expected. If using pots, plant carefully when the soil temperature reaches 70°F (21°C)—okra resents root disturbance—12 inches (30cm) apart. Cover with floating row covers to protect against wind until well established.

Care: Okra needs a deeply dug, fertile soil, but don't add manure—the nitrogen encourages excessive leaf growth. Once established, okra needs little attention and has few problems apart from soil-living nematodes, so remember to rotate the crop. It is drought tolerant, but in very dry spells, a weekly watering will improve the yield of pods.

Harvesting: Pick the pods regularly, every other day, when they reach about 3 inches (7.5cm) long. Some cultivars are tender up to 5 inches (12cm) long. Larger pods may be fibrous—add them to the compost pile. Picking regularly will ensure more pods are produced.

Some okra cultivars have spiny leaves, so wear gloves.

Tomatillo / Okra

Tomato

Tomato

Refreshing, juicy fruit in a variety of shapes and sizes

Even if you only have space for a modest container, you can grow a tomato plant without much effort in any hardiness zone. With more garden space, you can easily grow enough to supply fresh tomatoes all summer, with enough to preserve, dry, or freeze for all winter, too. Choose several cultivars, considering a combination of plant growth habit, fruit size and color, and how you intend to eat them.

When to sow: In warm areas, wait until the soil temperature reaches at least 70°F (21°C). In the coldest areas, start seeds indoors, about eight weeks before the last expected frost, where you can maintain a steady 70°F (21°C).

How to sow: To start from seeds from your own disease-free plants, just throw a couple of over-ripe fruit on the ground and look forward to seedlings. Plant transplants deeply— extra roots are formed along buried stems, which gives the plant a boost. Bury so the lowest set of leaves are on the soil surface. Space bush plants 4 feet (1.2m) apart and vine types 2 feet (60cm) apart in rows, with 4 feet (1.2m) between rows.

Staking and training indeterminate tomatoes will increase their yield.

Make sure they don't shade adjacent plants. Tomatoes need a rich, well-drained soil, so work in compost or well-rotted organic matter before planting. To grow in a container, start with a 3-gallon (12.5L) or larger container and fill it with a rich potting mix. Choose either a dwarf determinate or bush cultivar to save work, but expect to harvest over a relatively short season.

Care: To help warm up the soil, cover the rows with black plastic sheets. You can plant through cross-shape slits. In cold areas, cover newly planted transplants with floating row covers until they are well established. Water the plants regularly to keep the soil uniformly moist at the roots, otherwise fruit problems can develop later. A drip irrigation system is a good investment. Feed regularly with a balanced or high-potassium fertilizer— too much nitrogen will produce excess foliage. Bush, or determinate, cultivars don't need any pruning or training,

but they do benefit from support. The easiest way to support them is to cage them. Indeterminate types will need supporting; a single wooden stake is simplest, or two other good options are to use a tepee of poles with one plant trained to each pole or a trellis using wire or plastic mesh stretched between posts.

Harvesting: Once the skin reaches its mature color, the fruit is ready to harvest. Pick ripe fruit every other day when they are in full flow. If unripe fruit are left on the plants when the first fall frosts are due, pick them; then bring indoors and put them on a sunny windowsill to continue ripening.

Recommended types and cultivars:
Bushy, compact determinate types produce fruit for about six weeks. Unruly indeterminate types keep growing until killed by frost. These are best pruned to a single stem.

Beefsteaks produce huge, meaty fruit, weighing up to 1 pound (450g) each, especially if you thin them so there is only one fruit per bunch.

Cherry tomatoes produce long strings or bunches of small, sweet fruit. They are the ideal choice for growing in containers and are a treat eaten straight from the bush.

Pear-, plum-, and grape-shape tomatoes have a sweet flavor but meaty texture. The fruits may be red, yellow, or orange and are produced on indeterminate plants.

Heirloom tomatoes come in a variety of shapes, flavors, and colors. These grow on either semideterminate or indeterminate plants.

Semideterminate types produce short vines but bear fruit over a longer period than determinate types. There's a huge choice of tomatoes, including giant beefsteaks, slicing tomatoes, tiny cherry tomatoes, paste tomatoes, and pear tomatoes.
- 'Better Boy', a beefsteak type, bears red, 1-pound (450g) fruit on indeterminate plants (72 days).
- 'Big Beef' is a modern indeterminate beefsteak with an old-fashioned flavor. The fruit weigh up to 1 pound (450g) each. Disease resistant and suitable for all areas (73 days).
- 'Celebrity', a hybrid slicing-tomato cultivar, bears heavy yields of 7-ounce (200g) red fruit on determinate plants; good disease resistance (70 days).
- 'Early Girl', an early slicing tomato, has red fruit weighing 6 ounces (170g) each, on indeterminate plants (52 days).
- 'Husky Gold' is a midsize slicing tomato, with 6-ounce (170g) golden fruit on dwarf indeterminate vines; good disease resistance (70 days).

- 'Juliet' is a cherry-tomato cultivar with red fruit produced on indeterminate plants (70 days).
- 'Micro Tom' is a tiny determinate type with plants growing just 6–8 inches (15–20cm) high; it is good in containers or hanging baskets (88 days).
- 'Oregon Spring' is a slicing tomato with early and heavy crops of 6-ounce (170g) red fruit, even in the North (60 days).
- 'Sugary', a cherry-tomato plant, produces small, bright red, grape-shaped fruit that hang in bunches on semideterminate plants (60 days).
- 'Sungold', an early cultivar with orange fruit, is one of the sweetest cherry tomatoes (57 days).
- 'Supersweet 100' is a prolific, indeterminate cherry type with good disease resistance (65 days).
- Paste tomatoes bear elongated, fleshy fruit with strong flavors; grow them for canning, sauces, and paste. 'Roma VF', 'San Marzano', and 'Viva Italia' produce fruit weighing 3 ounces (85g) each on determinate plants (76–80 days).

Cucumber

Refreshing, crisp salad staple

Cucumbers can be rampant vining plants, so grow them on trellises, or try modern bush cultivars that are small enough for a container and will still produce plenty of normal-size fruit. And if you grow pickling types, you can enjoy the pickled version all through winter, too.

When to sow: Whether you sow directly or plant transplants, wait until the soil is a steady 65°F (18°C).

How to sow: In warm areas, sow seeds directly into the soil. In cool areas with a short growing season, start seeds in individual pots indoors, where you can maintain a temperature of 70°F (21°C). Leave the plants outdoors longer each day so they get used to cooler temperatures before planting them outside. Growing the plants in "hills" of mounded soil improves drainage. Add plenty of compost to make hills 6 inches (15cm) high and 4 feet (1.2m) apart. Sow six seeds per hill; thin to the best three.

Care: Cucumbers need full sun and rich, well-drained soil. Work an inch (2.5cm) or so of well-rotted manure

The fruit will form behind the plant's large, attractive yellow or orange blossoms.

into the soil before planting or sowing. In cool areas, cover the soil with a black plastic sheet a few weeks before transplanting to help warm it. In all areas, water the soil thoroughly and cover with black plastic or mulch to retain moisture and suppress weeds. Water regularly—a drip irrigation system is ideal—and feed regularly, too, with a balanced or high-potassium fertilizer. To prevent powdery mildew from developing, grow plants on a trellis for better air circulation.

Harvesting: Pick cucumbers young. Check the plants every other day and cut pickle cultivars when 3–4 inches (7.5–10cm) long and slicing types when 6–8 inches (15–20cm) long. Don't let cucumbers reach full size and start producing seeds, or the crop will dwindle. Pickling cultivars crop over a short period, but slicers should keep going for weeks.

Recommended cultivars:
Choose a bush cultivar for growing in containers. For pickling, look for a cultivar that produces small fruit.
• 'Alibi', with fruit up to 4 inches (10cm) long on compact vines, is suitable for pickling (55 days).
• 'Armenian' is an unusual cultivar with pale green, ribbed fruit with a mild, sweet flavor (70 days)
• 'Burpee Pickler', a pickling cultivar, produces a prolific crop over a long season (53 days).
• 'Bush Champion' is a compact, bushy plant that bears a heavy crop (55 days).
• 'Diva', an all-female slicing cultivar, provides a big yield of sweet, thin-skinned fruit (58 days).
• 'Fanfare' is a compact slicing vine with fruit 8–9-inches (20–23cm) long (63 days).
• 'Lemon' has sweet round, yellow fruit, 3–4 inches (7.5–10cm) across; good for salads or pickled (65 days).
• 'Salad Bush' bears normal-size (8-inch/20cm) fruit on compact bush plants (57 days).
• 'Straight Eight', a slicing cultivar, has fruit 8 inches (20cm) long with good flavor (58 days).

Pinch off the vines when they reach the top of a trellis to encourage sideshoots.

Some melons have smooth skin, others textured skin.

Melon

Juicy, refreshing summertime treat

Once you've experienced the full flavor of homegrown melons and learned to gauge when they are at their peak of perfection, you won't want to be without at least one plant in the plot. Thanks to early-ripening, more-compact cultivars, melon can now be grown in all hardiness zones as long as you choose the right cultivars.

When to sow: Don't rush sowing seeds or planting transplants outdoors. In northern and cold areas, start seeds indoors in individual pots. Maintain a temperature of at least 70°F (21°C). Delay planting outdoors until the soil temperature is at least 65°F (18°C). Acclimatize the plants by leaving them outdoors longer each day before planting. In warm areas, as long as the soil is 65°F (18°C) and it is within two weeks of the last expected frost date, you can sow the seeds directly in the ground.

How to sow: Melons are large plants that need plenty of room to grow and a rich, well-drained soil. Work in a layer of compost before planting. In warm areas, plant in "hills" of mounded soil, 6 feet (1.8m) apart for trailing watermel-ons, 5 feet (1.5m) apart for trailing melons, and 3–4 feet (90–120cm) apart for bush types. Sow six seeds per hill; thin to the best three seedlings later.

Care: Melons need plenty of water, at least an inch (2.5cm) per week. However, withholding water for about a week before harvesting should increase the sweetness of the fruit. Support fruit on trellised plants with slings made of plastic mesh, such as an old onion bag, attached to the trellis. Place a board, tile, or upturned pot under the fruit of trailing plants to keep them off the soil. In cool areas, cover the young plants with floating row covers to keep them warm and protect them from insects.

Harvesting: Judging the precise moment to cut fully ripe melons can be tricky. Key indicators are when the blossom end feels slightly soft, when the skin color changes, and when the last leaf before the fruit turns pale. Melons also give off a sweet fragrance when ripe. Muskmelons will detach from the vine, but they are best if cut off just before this happens. Watermelons give off a dull sound when thumped, and the base, where it rests on the soil, should be fully colored. Melons will keep for a week or two uncut in a cool place.

Recommended types and cultivars:
• Charantais are small French melons with orange flesh and green or gray skin. 'Edonis' (70 days) and 'Honey Girl' (75 days) have typical 2-pound (900g) fruit.
• Crenshaw types bear large oval melons with yellow skin and pale green or salmon flesh. 'Burpee Early Sweet' has 15-pound (6.8kg) fruit with pink flesh and is early enough for all zones (85–90 days).
• Galia has green netted skin and pale green flesh with a subtle flavor. 'Passport' bears 5-pound (2.3kg) fruit and is suited to all areas (73 days).
• Honeydews are winter melons that have smooth, round fruit with white skin and flesh that is green, white, pink, or orange. 'Early Dew' has 3-pound (1.4kg) fruit with pale green flesh (75 days); 'Orange Sorbet' has 7–8-pound (3.2–3.6kg) fruit with pale orange flesh (82 days).
• Muskmelon, also called cantaloupe, has orange flesh with a musty, sweet flavor and netted skin. 'Ambrosia' has small 5-pound (2.3kg) fruit with firm, pale orange flesh (90 days).
• Spanish melons bear 4-pound (1.8kg) fruit with smooth yellow skin and pale green flesh. 'Amy' has smaller fruit with white flesh (70 days).
• Watermelons are available as bush cultivars that produce small melons at 5 pounds (2.3kg), icebox types with manageable vines, or the classic huge melons weighing 20 pounds (9kg) or more. 'Crimson Sweet' has large, red-flesh fruit on disease-resistant plants (85 days). 'Moon and Stars' is an heirloom with large green fruit splashed with yellow (100 days). 'Sugar Baby' is a good cultivar with medium-size, red-flesh fruit (80 days).

Pumpkin & Winter Squash

The giants of the garden

Pumpkins and winter squash are heat-loving vegetables that need a long growing season.

When to sow: In warm areas, sow the seeds directly into the soil, 1–2 inches (2.5–5cm) deep. Wait until a couple of weeks after the last expected spring frost or until the soil temperature is above 60°F (16°C). In cold areas, start the seeds indoors, where you can maintain a temperature of 70°F (21°C).

How to sow: If sowing seeds directly, sow up to four seeds per planting position, and thin later to the strongest two seedlings. If starting indoors, sow seeds individually in pots. Sow seeds or plant transplants 3–4 feet (90–120cm) apart each way for bush and semitrailing types and 5–6 feet (1.5–1.8m) apart for vining types. Pumpkins and squash need rich, well-drained soil. Traditionally, they are grown on "hills." Before mounding the soil, mix in a generous amount of well-rotted manure. Covering the bed with a black plastic sheet will help warm the soil and suppress weeds, which can be difficult to control once the vines are growing rapidly. Cut circles in the plastic for the mounds. If space is limited, use trellis supports for cultivars with smaller fruit and train them upward. Be careful they do not shade your other crops.

Care: Give the area a good soaking every week to wet the soil deeply. When four to six healthy pumpkins or squashes form on a plant, prune the shoot tips and remove any other fruit. The plant will concentrate its energy on producing less, but better-tasting, fruit.

Harvesting: Leave the fruit outside as long as possible to ripen fully. If necessary, prune the leaves to expose the mature fruit to the sun. Always cut the vine on either side of the fruit stalk, leaving the fruit stalk intact. In cool areas, move ripe pumpkins or squashes to a sunny, sheltered spot to complete their ripening. Then move them to a warm place indoors (85°F/29°C) to cure for a week.

Both pumpkins and winter squash have hard, inedible rinds that protect the often sweet flesh inside.

Recommended types and cultivars:
There are many types of winter squash.
• Pumpkins don't develop as hard a rind as other winter squash do. Small pumpkins have sweet, rich orange flesh for eating. 'Baby Bear' has 1½–2½-pound (0.7–1.1kg) fruit just right for a pie (105 days). 'Dill's Atlantic Giant' is the one to grow if size matters (120 days). 'Orange Smoothy' bears 6–9-pound (2.7–4kg) fruit good for eating or carving.
• Acorn squashes bear medium-size, ridged fruit for baking. These bush plants are useful where space is limited. 'Table Ace' fruit weighs 2 pounds (900g) and has dark green skin and sweet orange flesh (75 days).

• Butternut squashes have club-shaped fruit with the seeds in the bulbous end and a solid neck of orange flesh. 'Waltham' has uniform 3–4-pound (1.4–1.8kg) fruit with solid flesh (85 days).
• Hubbard types grow fruit pointed at both ends, with blue-gray warty skin and orange flesh. 'Blue Hubbard' is up to 10 pounds (4.5kg) and stores well (110 days).
• Kabocha types produce medium-size, round, flattened fruit that stores well and has a rich flavor (95 days).
• Spaghetti squash is baked or boiled whole (making sure to prick the skin first). When split open, the flesh is forked out and looks like spaghetti. Most are trailing plants, but modern cultivars have a bush habit (75 days).

Zucchini & Summer Squash

Thin-skinned vegetable with a mild flesh

These are compact and productive plants with vigorous bushes—two or three plants should be plenty.

When to sow: In warm areas, wait until a few weeks after the last frost date and the soil temperature is 60°F (16°C).

How to sow: Prepare planting "hills," working in plenty of compost and mounding the soil. Push three or four seeds into the top; thin them later to the strongest two seedlings. In cold areas, start seeds in 3–4-inch (7.5–10cm) pots four weeks before the last frost date. Meanwhile, warm the soil by covering it with black plastic sheets. Plant them outdoors when the soil temperature is at least 60°F (16°C), but first leave the seedlings outside longer each day to get used to the temperature. To reduce weeds, plant through cross-shaped slits in the plastic, 3 feet (90cm) apart.

Care: Cover plants with floating row covers to prevent most insect pests, and take precautions against slugs. Don't let summer squash run out of water; they need the equivalent of an inch (2.5cm) of rain each week. Install a drip irrigation system to save a lot of work. Feed regularly with a high-potassium fertilizer. Remove the covers when flowers appear so that they will be pollinated.

Harvesting: The only rule is to keep picking and never let any fruit get too big. The ideal size is 6 inches (15cm) for the long ones and 2–3 inches (5–7.5cm) for round ones.

Recommended types and cultivars:
• Crookneck squashes have a kink toward the top of the fruit. Cultivars include 'Early Summer Crookneck' and 'Pic' n' Pic' (50 days).

Pollination
Squashes produce both male and female flowers (with females having a slight bulge beneath them); however, your plants may be producing only male flowers early in the season. Cold weather or a lack of pollinating insects may mean female flowers are present but just not being fertilized. You can hand pollinate to ensure fruit will develop; use a cotton swab to collect pollen from the male flowers and to deposit it in the females.

• Patty Pan types have flattened fruit with scalloped edges. 'Peter Pan' has pale green fruit; 'Sunburst' has yellow fruit (50–55 days).
• Straightneck types have clublike, warty yellow fruit. Pick up to 8 inches (20cm) long. 'Saffron' is typical (45 days).
• Zucchini are all compact plants producing fruit in many colors: 'Black Beauty' is dark green, 'Gold Rush' yellow, and 'Magda' cream (45–50 days).

Club-shaped but with a crook near the top, crookneck squash grow from the end of the blossom.

When cutting the fruit with a sharp knife, leave 1 in. (2.5cm) of the stem attached to the fruit.

Basil

A Mediterranean favorite

The warm, pungent aroma of fresh basil features in many recipes. There are several variations on the typical basil grown for cooking, such as selections with purple foliage and those with a lemon scent or more spicy flavors.

When to sow: Sow indoors four to six weeks before the last expected spring frost.

How to sow: Basil is tender, and its leaves turn black at the slightest frost. Growth can slow down in cool weather. The best way to grow basil is to sow a small amount of seeds every few weeks. Put a few seeds in a 3-inch (8cm) pot of seed-starting mix. Keep at 75°F (24°C) until they germinate, usually within two weeks. Let them continue to grow; acclimatize the young plants to cooler conditions gradually. Basil is more successful in a small container, but you can sow directly in the ground. Wait until the soil temperature is at least 60°F (15.5°C). Once there is no danger of frost, plant transplants 12 inches (30cm) apart for large types, 6 inches (15cm) for dwarf types.

Care: Choose a warm, sheltered spot with moist but well-drained soil; avoid cold, damp sites, which will encourage

There are scores of varieties of aromatic basil.

fungal disease. Keep the soil moist, and protect plants from slugs. Liquid feed with a balanced fertilizer to encourage lush leaf growth. Pinch off growing tips to encourage a bushy habit. Plants that drop leaves or suddenly wilt may be infected with *Fusarium* wilt. Pull and destroy infected plants.

Harvesting: Once plants are 5–6 inches (12.5–15cm) high, pick the young leaves from the top of the stems. This will encourage more leaves to grow and result in neat, bushy plants. Remove no more than one-third of the leaves at a time.

Bay

An evergreen herb with strongly aromatic leaves

Bay can be either a treelike shrub or an evergreen houseplant, depending on whether it survives the winter in the garden or stays indoors in a pot.

When to sow: Plants can be purchased year-round.

How to sow: You can buy bay plants as rooted cuttings, small or large container plants, or clipped and trained topiary specimens. Prices can vary greatly, with topiary types being the most expensive.

Care: In warm areas, where temperatures don't drop below 10°F (-12°C), grow as an evergreen hedge or a large shrub. The ideal is a warm, sheltered spot in well-drained soil. Where frost is a factor, grow bay in a container so the plant can be outdoors in summer and moved indoors in winter. You can clip large plants into shape in summer.

Harvesting: Simply pick off the leaves as required for soups or sauces. Bay is evergreen, so the leaves are available year-round. There is no need to dry them unless you have surplus from clipping trained plants in summer.

Simply pluck a bay leaf for flavoring a soup or stew.

Chervil

An unusual annual with an anise flavor

Fresh chervil can perk up a bland salad. It has finely divided leaves that resemble parsley. When dried, it can be used as an ingredient for a bouquet garni.

When to sow: Spring

How to sow: Buy fresh seeds each spring, and sow where the plant is to grow—chervil doesn't transplant well. Sow small amounts every three weeks or so. Early sowings will send up flower stalks rapidly; later sowings will continue until killed by frost. (In mild climate areas, late sowings may survive over the winter.) Sow thinly, and thin out the seedlings to 6–8 inches (15–20cm) apart.

Care: Chervil prefers a shady position in moist soil. Keep this herb well watered, or it will send up flower stalks even more quickly, especially when grown in a container.

Chervil is a delicate springtime herb.

Harvesting: Pick the leaves any time before the flowers start to open. You can start picking leaves early to help delay flowering.

Chives

Perennial member of the onion family

One of the easiest herbs to grow, chives have edible hollow leaves with a mild onion flavor and pretty mauve flowers that can also be eaten. An alternative is garlic chives, with a flavor between onion and garlic.

When to sow: Year-round, but usually early spring to summer

How to sow: Sow seeds indoors in pots or directly in the ground outside. These will be slow to grow, so allow a year before harvesting. A faster option is to buy plants, or get a friend to donate clumps. Thin seedlings or plant clumps 6–8 inches (15–20cm) apart.

Care: Chives grow in sun or partial shade in dry or moist soil. The leaves die back in winter in cold climates; in warm areas, they are evergreen. Fork in some organic matter before planting; water until the plants are growing well. If your plants turn yellow, cut them back to a 2-inch (5cm) stump. Water well if conditions are dry, and fresh new foliage should appear. If plants become congested, the quality of the leaves will deteriorate. In spring or fall, lift crowded clumps from the ground, gently easing them out with a garden fork. Split the clumps into fist-size sections, each with roots and healthy tops. Replant the healthiest sections, and discard the rest.

Harvesting: If you snip off the tips of the leaves, unsightly brown marks will appear at the top of the plant. Instead, use scissors to cut the leaves further down, leaving a 2-inch (5cm) stump to regrow. Stop harvesting three weeks before the first frost date. To use the flowers, pick them fresh; break up the flower heads into smaller parts; and scatter them over a salad.

Chives add a subtle onion flavor to foods.

Cilantro & Coriander

Flavorful seeds and refreshing leaves

Both the leaves and seeds of coriander can be used in cooking. The fresh young leaves, known as cilantro, are widely used in Asian and Mexican dishes, while the seeds, called coriander, are used as a spice.

When to sow: Year-round but usually spring and fall

How to sow: Cilantro is an annual plant that does not transplant well. Sow the seeds directly into their final position. This can be either into the ground in rows or scattered into a large container. Sow the seeds every two weeks to ensure that you have a continuous supply, but stop during hot weather. Sow seeds 1 inch (2.5cm) deep and 2 inches (5cm) apart, and thin the seedlings to 6–8 inches (15–20cm).

Care: Cilantro will grow in sun or partial shade in normal soil that has been enriched with some organic matter to keep it moist. Once the hot weather and long days of summer arrive, the plants will quickly form flower stalks. The white flowers are a magnet for beneficial insects. Although the plants will slow down their leaf production, the flowers will set seed and dry out, and you'll be able to use these plants to harvest the seeds.

Cilantro is widely used in Latin and Asian cuisines.

Harvesting: Start cutting leaves when the plants are about 6 inches (15cm) or so high. You can chop cilantro leaves and scatter them onto salads or use them in Mexican or Indian dishes. Use fine-leafed cultivars whole. Seed heads will ripen in late summer and fall to the ground; cut them before this happens once they turn brown. Place in a paper bag, and dry in a warm, airy place. When completely dry, store the seeds in airtight jars.

Recommended cultivars:
• 'Delfino' has finely divided leaves that make it an attractive garnish.
• 'Leisure', often described as slow to send up flower stalks, is one of the cultivars bred for leaf production.

Fennel

A tall, elegant plant

Fennel for the herb garden has the same aniseed flavor and feathery foliage as the vegetable Florence fennel, but not the bulb-like base. You can use the foliage as an herb, and also harvest the seeds.

When to sow: Spring or fall

How to sow: Sow seeds directly into the ground in spring in cold areas or in fall in southern gardens, when temperatures are 60–65°F (15.5–18°C).

Care: Fennel prefers moist, deep soil so that its taproot has plenty of room, but it copes well in free-draining soils, too. Pick a 2 × 2-foot (60 × 60cm) sunny spot. In mild climates where seeds can survive the winter, remove the flowers after they've formed seed heads but before they shed their seeds to prevent spreading.

Harvesting: Cut leaves when they are large enough to use. Gather the seeds when the seed heads are dry and turn brown. Fennel will self seed; if that is a problem, cut off the flowers. Do not grow fennel near dill because they will cross-pollinate and produce inferior seedlings.

Fennel's seeds and feathery leaves are used in cooking.

Lemon Balm

A member of the mint family

As its name implies, the leaves have a hint of lemon flavor.

When to sow: Spring

How to sow: You can buy a plant from a garden center, but lemon balm is easy to grow from seeds. Sow either indoors in a pot or directly outdoors into the garden soil. Germination can take three weeks.

Care: Lemon balm will grow in most situations and soils. In hot areas, provide some shade from midday sun, particularly for the yellow and variegated forms. Cut down old foliage, and lift and divide the plant in the fall. In warm areas, this herb is a perennial and will self seed.

Harvesting: Simply cut or pinch off leaves as needed. The flavor of the leaves is best before the plant flowers.

Use lemon balm to make a soothing, hot tea.

If the quality of the leaves is poor, cut back to 2 inches (5cm) above soil level; water; and then wait for a fresh flush of young foliage to appear. You can pick some lemon balm leaves to make a refreshing tea.

Lemongrass

A tufted perennial with thick stems

A popular ingredient in Asian cooking, lemongrass *(Cymbopogon citratus)* has aromatic leaves and lemon-flavored leaf bases. These parts of the plant are used in a variety of dishes, from soups to curries, and are added to spice mixes.

Lemongrass is an essential flavor in many Asian dishes.

When to sow: Buy a plant in spring.

How to sow: Lemongrass rarely flowers, so it is difficult to grow from seeds. Purchase young plants from a garden center. Grow lemongrass in a container because it can be invasive in mild areas. Move the plant indoors during winter in all but the warmest areas; it is hardy only in Zones 9 to 11. Choose a container 12 inches (30cm) wide, and fill it with a potting mix. Alternatively, divide an established clump, and replant the divisions.

Care: Grow in full sun in a warm spot that is sheltered from wind. Keep well watered in summer, and give it a balanced liquid fertilizer. Move plants indoors in winter, and keep them just moist. Eventually, the plants can become congested and will need dividing. Tip them out of their pots to divide the clumps, and make sure each divided section has roots and healthy leaves. Replant the healthiest sections into containers filled with fresh potting mix, and discard the rest.

Harvesting: Detach young stems from the plant, and remove the leaves to reveal a stalk with a thick base. Gently crush the base, and add to soups, stews, or curries. The tender inner parts of the lemongrass leaf bases can also be used raw and should be finely sliced or pounded to make a paste. The stalks are sometimes used as skewers for seafood.

Lemon Balm / Lemongrass

Marjoram

A relative of oregano

Although a perennial, marjoram *(Origanum majorana)* is sometimes treated as an annual herb. Marjoram has a sweeter, more subtle flavor than oregano.

When to sow: Spring

How to sow: You can raise marjoram each year from seeds, but it is slow to get going. It is easier to buy a plant from a garden center. Marjoram can also be propagated easily from cuttings. Marjoram is hardy up to Zone 6, where it can be treated as a perennial; in cool areas, treat it as an annual. Space plants about 8 inches (20cm) apart.

Care: Marjoram requires poor, well-drained soil, so it is a good candidate for a container. Before flowering starts, trim the plant back to encourage fresh growth.

Harvesting: Pick young shoots regularly to keep the plant neat. Dry marjoram for winter use. Strip off the leaves as needed.

Related to oregano, marjoram has a subtler flavor.

Mint

A highly aromatic herb

While refreshing as a tea or flavoring, mints are also attractive plants and have a lot to offer the cook and gardener. They are herbaceous perennials, so plants will last for years. Spearmint and peppermint are the most useful in the kitchen, but there are many other types, such as the milder apple mint, with its attractive woolly leaves, and the eye-catching variegated ginger mint. Mint's lush, green leaves make it an attractive container plant.

When to sow: Buy a plant in spring.

How to sow: Buy a small plant, or get a few pieces of underground stem. Plant in a large container in a rich potting mix—simply inserting cuttings just below the soil surface will be sufficient. Mint can be invasive, so it is best grown in a raised bed where the roots can be confined or in containers sunk into the soil with 2 inches (5cm) of the rim aboveground.

Care: Keep plants well watered, and feed them with a balanced liquid fertilizer. If grown in a container, you can keep mint in partial shade or full sun. Remove flowers as soon as they form to prevent seeding.

Harvesting: Mints are vigorous plants, so you can start harvesting as soon as new growth emerges. Later, cut off the top half of the young stems, and strip off the leaves. For fresh mint over winter, tip the plant out of its pot, and select some runners to cut from the parent plant. Use a fresh container, and cover the plant with 1 inch (2.5cm) of potting mix. Water and keep it in a cool, well-ventilated place.

Vigorous mint plants should be grown in containers.

Oregano adds flavor to Mediterranean cuisines.

Oregano

A favorite for tomato dishes

The leaves of oregano *(Origanum vulgare),* which is a perennial, add flavor to Mediterranean dishes. There are both Greek and Italian species.

When to sow: Buy plants in spring or fall.

How to sow: Raising plants from seeds can provide variable results, so buy potted plants from a garden center; take divisions in the fall or stem cuttings in the spring or fall. Oregano varies in flavor, so before choosing a plant to purchase, rub a leaf to release its flavor and then taste it.

Care: Oregano thrives in full sun and in well-drained soil, and dwarf types are suitable for containers. Oregano may not survive really cold winters; digging up small plants and keeping them in pots on a sunny windowsill over winter is an option. If top growth becomes poor, cut back all stems to within 2 inches (5cm) of the ground in summer to encourage fresh growth.

Harvesting: Pick leaves as soon as the young plants are established. Regular harvesting will encourage a bushy shape. Once the plant starts flowering, the flavor will diminish. For larger quantities, cut back plants when they are about 6 inches (15cm) tall, again before they flower, and finally in late summer. After each cutting, there will be fresh growth.

Parsley

A great standby in the kitchen

Gardeners often treat parsley as a hardy annual because the best leaves for the kitchen are produced in the first year. There are two types: the strong-flavored, tight, curly parsley and the sweeter, flat-leaf, or Italian, parsley.

When to sow: Early summer

How to sow: Parsley is easy to grow from seeds. Parsley seeds need two to four weeks to germinate, during which time the soil must be constantly moist. Sow seeds directly into the ground when the soil temperature is at least 50°F (10°C). Grow in rows 10 inches (25cm) apart, and thin plants to 8 inches (20cm) apart.

Care: Parsley does better in cool, partial shade and in fertile, moist soil. Protect it with a floating row cover to keep insects away. Mud splashes can spoil parsley, particularly the curly types. Look for cultivars with long stems, or mulch around the plants. Keep the mulch an inch (2.5cm) away from the stems to avoid crown rot, and water the plants carefully to avoid splashing.

Harvesting: Start to cut leaves when the plants are about 6 inches (15cm) tall. Cut the stems 1–2 inches (2.5–5cm) above the crown so the plants can produce more leaves. The stalks have a lot of flavor but can be tough, so use these for stocks and soups. If you need a lot of parsley, cut the whole plant.

Parsley grows best in partial shade.

Oregano / Parsley

Rosemary

A tender, evergreen shrub

Rosemary has needlelike leaves, pale blue flowers, a strong flavor, and a distinctive aroma. It is hardy only in Zones 8 to 10; elsewhere, treat the plant as an annual.

When to sow: Buy a plant in spring.

How to sow: Buy a plant, or ask a friend for some cuttings (taken in mid- to late summer). Plant outdoors in spring in light, well-drained soil—fork in some gravel or sand to improve the drainage if the soil needs it. Keep moist until the roots are established. Alternatively, choose a dwarf cultivar and grow it in a container of free-draining potting soil; in winter, bring the plant indoors and keep it well lit (with 4 hours each day of direct sunlight or 12 hours of artificial light).

Rosemary is a strongly aromatic herb.

Care: In mild areas with well-drained soil, rosemary is care-free. If the plant isn't thriving, give it a side-dressing of compost. Brown leaves indicate overwatering. In containers, water only when the soil is moderately dry.

Harvesting: Pinch the stem tips for some fresh leaves—this will also keep the plant bushy. On mature plants, remove a few branches—this will provide a supply of leaves that you can freeze or dry and will improve the shape.

Sage

A herb full of aroma even when dried

The sage *(Salvia officinalis)* that cooks use is a perennial and is hardy in Zones 4 to 8. Although not as stunning as ornamental sages, culinary sage has cultivars with attractive purple, green, or variegated leaves that make them suitable foliage plants for an ornamental garden.

When to sow: Buy a plant in spring.

How to sow: It is easier to start with a small plant in spring. Seed-raised plants need two years before harvesting, and the cultivars with the most attractive foliage are grown from cuttings. Plant in well-drained soil in a sunny position.

Care: As perennials, sage plants fit in better in perennial borders than in a vegetable patch. In warm zones, sage grows as an evergreen shrub—the main limiting factor is waterlogged soil over winter, so containers or raised beds are a useful alternative. Cut back young specimens by one-third each spring to stimulate fresh growth.

Harvesting: Because sage has a strong flavor, you should use only a few leaves at a time—simply pluck them off the plant. Sage leaves will dry well.

Culinary sage may have green or purple leaves.

Savory

A substitute for ground pepper

There are two types of savory: summer savory *(Satureja hortensis),* an annual herb with thin leaves and small pink flowers, and winter savory *(S. montana),* a spreading perennial with narrow leaves that is hardy in Zones 5 to 9. Choose between summer or winter savory, or grow both types for year-round use. Both types of savory will add a peppery flavor to bean, cheese, and egg dishes, but winter savory has a slightly stronger flavor.

When to sow: Spring to summer

How to sow: Sow the annual summer savory or the perennial winter savory where they will grow in spring. Thin plants to 8 inches (20cm) apart for summer savory, 12 inches (30cm) for winter savory. You can also grow winter savory from cuttings.

Care: Savory will tolerate hot, dry conditions and poor soil. Summer savory can be grown in the vegetable garden; winter savory is best in an herb bed but is attactive enough for an ornamental border. You can cut back established winter savory plants to stop them from sprawling and to encourage fresh healthy growth.

Savory's peppery flavor pairs well with eggs and cheese.

Harvesting: Pick leaves as needed once the plants reach 6 inches (15cm) tall. When summer savory has flowered, cut the whole plant and dry it for winter use. Continue picking winter savory in winter—it is better fresh. (It becomes hard when dried.) Use fresh summer savory to flavor fava beans and meats. Winter savory is a good substitute for thyme or rosemary.

Tarragon needs well-drained soil and full sun.

Tarragon

A perennial with a subtle licorice flavor

Tarragon *(Artemisia dracunculus),* also called French tarragon, will do best in areas with cool summers and a distinct dormant period.

When to sow: Buy a plant in spring.

How to sow: Tarragon does not produce seeds, so you'll need to buy a plant. Don't confuse the culinary *A. dracunculus* with Russian tarragon *(A. dracunculus* var. *dracunculoides),* which has a coarser flavor. If plants are not labeled, they are likely to be the former. Give the plant 12 inches (30cm) to itself.

Care: Tarragon requires well-drained soil and full sun, which makes it a good container plant. Or grow it in a raised bed with other drought-tolerant herbs, such as thyme. Each summer, as it starts to flower, cut back the top growth to encourage fresh leaves. In cold areas, cover with straw to protect it over winter. A plant takes a year or two to mature; harvest lightly until it is established. After a few years the clump may become congested. Dig it up; remove some pieces of younger roots with shoots attached; and replant them.

Harvesting: Cut or pinch off the top third of the stems. Use the leaves fresh or to flavor vinegar.

Thyme

A shrubby perennial with tiny leaves

There are hundreds of thymes, but most cooks opt for common thyme, which imparts a warm, spicy flavor to meat, cheese, egg, and pasta dishes.

When to sow: Spring

How to sow: You can raise some types from seeds, but it is easier to start with small plants in spring. Plant in well-drained soil or potting mix in sun or partial shade.

Care: Thymes are neat in habit but can get swamped by more vigorous herbs. In a rock garden or on top of a wall are locations worth considering. Low-growing, matlike thymes can be tricky to harvest, but growing them in raised beds, hanging baskets, or window boxes makes harvesting easier—and the leaves should be less muddy. Plant 6–12 inches (15–30cm) apart, and shear back after flowering to keep them bushy.

Harvesting: Cut off some stems, and remove the leaves in the kitchen. Thyme dries well.

Thyme grows well in raised beds and window boxes.

Globe Artichoke

A distinctive gourmet vegetable

Globe artichokes need plenty of space, but they are worthy of a place in the flower border. They are hardy to Zone 7; in cold regions, grow them as annuals.

When to sow: Spring

How to sow: For a perennial crop in warm areas, buy young plants of a good strain. Globe artichokes are easy to grow from seeds. This is the best option in cool areas where they are grown as an annual crop. Sow seeds ½ inch (1.3cm) deep in 3-inch (7.5cm) pots about 8 to 12 weeks before the last spring frost. They germinate best at around 75°F (24°C). If necessary, transfer them into 4-inch (10cm) pots. Plant in their final positions outdoors after the last frost date. In cold regions, the temperature should remain below 50°F (10°C) for ten days—this tricks the plant into flowering in its first year instead of producing only leaves.

Care: Dig or rototill the area deeply, adding plenty of organic material and removing any weeds at the same time. Allow 3–4 feet (90–120cm) between plants and 5–6 feet (1.5–1.8m) between rows as a perennial crop, and 2–3 feet (60–90cm) apart as an annual crop. Cut perennial plants to ground level after harvesting the buds; they will resprout soon afterward. If the plants become dense clumps, divide them so each division has at least two buds. In late fall, cut plants to ground level; cover with mulch.

Harvesting: Perennial plantings produce a crop in spring with a smaller crop in the fall each year. Those grown as annuals will crop once in the fall. Cut the flower buds when they are full size and still firm, and the lowest scales just start to open. After cooking, discard the "choke," which is the immature flower. The fleshy base beneath and the bases of the scales are what you eat.

Globe artichokes are easy to grow from seeds.

Asparagus

Fresh, tasty spears

Asparagus is not a crop for the impatient—you'll have to wait two years for the first taste, and three years before you have a decent crop. Even then, the season lasts only six to eight weeks. However, once it starts cropping, it should continue for many years with little work on your part, except for weeding between plants.

When to sow: Plant asparagus in spring or fall—spring is best for cool areas, fall for warm areas.

How to sow: You can grow asparagus from seeds, but because it takes three years until you get your first crop, most people start with 1-year-old crowns—the underground stem base and roots. Because asparagus is such a long-term crop, spend some time getting the soil right. Asparagus prefers a light, free-draining soil with a neutral pH (6.5–7.5); add lime if your soil is more acidic. Dig a trench 6–8 inches (15–20cm) deep and 12 inches (30cm) wide. Make a ridge of compost down the center of the trench. Space the crowns 18 inches (45cm) apart, straddling the ridge of compost so their roots spread down either side. If you want more than one row, space them at least 3 feet (90cm) apart.

Care: The major work involved in growing asparagus is keeping the weeds under control. Mulch with a weed-free compost of other organic material around the plants. Water newly established beds regularly—setting up a drip irrigation system is most efficient. After two years, the plants will take care of themselves. Feed the plants in late spring or early summer when you stop cutting. Apply a balanced fertilizer, or dress with compost. Leave the ferns until they die back completely after a couple of hard frosts. Then cut them to about 12 inches (30cm) from soil level, and mulch the rows. You can pull out the dry stems in spring.

Harvesting: In the first year, don't be tempted to pick any spears. Let them all grow into ferny fronds to help build up the crowns. In the second year, you can cut spears for a limited period, but after a month, let the fronds grow. In the third year, you can start to harvest for a full six to eight weeks. Wait until the spears are 6–8 inches (15–20cm) tall and the tips are still tight. Snap them cleanly at soil level, or cut them with a knife just below soil level.

Recommended types and cultivars:
• 'Jersey' series, such as 'Jersey Knight' and 'Jersey Supreme', are rust-resistant, all-male cultivars—all-male types produce more spears.
• 'Purple Passion' is a hybrid, but not all-male; the purple spears are sweeter than green types.

Spread out the roots of the asparagus crowns when planting them in a trench.

Tender young asparagus spears, fresh from the garden, are a real treat in spring.

Horseradish / Jerusalem Artichoke

Horseradish is rarely attacked by pests.

Horseradish

Useful as a spicy condiment

This perennial is not related to the similarly named annual radishes, but it does have roots that are spicy hot. Horseradish is best confined to an unused corner of the vegetable garden, where it will provide roots without becoming a nuisance.

When to sow: Plant a root in spring.

How to sow: Horseradish is grown from pieces of root instead of seeds. If you need more than one plant, space the root cuttings at least 12 inches (30cm) apart. Cover with a mulch to suppress weeds and retain moisture.

Care: Except for watering early on if the soil gets dry, horseradish can be left unattended.

Harvesting: For the best flavor, wait until the plant has stopped actively growing and after the first few frosts before harvesting. Dig up the plant, and replant a sideshoot; trim off the top, and store the rest of the roots in a box of moist sand. If the ground doesn't freeze in your area, leave the plant in the ground and mulch it; dig roots as you need them until spring.

Jerusalem Artichoke

An American "sunflower"

These tall plants with their yellow flowers will make an effective barrier or screen during summer. The tubers have a texture similar to water chestnuts and a nutty taste. The roots are so prolific that, unless you gather every single one, they can become a real menace.

When to sow: Plant tubers in spring after the last expected frost date, or in fall four weeks before the first expected frost date.

How to sow: Instead of seeds, Jerusalem artichokes are normally grown from tubers. Although they will grow in any soil and even in partial shade, Jerusalem artichokes will do best in rich, well-drained soil. Give them room to grow by spacing the tubers 12 inches (30cm) apart, and bury them 4–6 inches (10–15cm) deep.

Care: Water the plants until established, and mulch to conserve soil moisture. Once established, they need no help. The plants will normally reappear the following year because it is difficult to remove all the tubers. In fact, they can become invasive if you aren't careful—don't inadvertently add pieces of root to the compost pile.

Harvesting: When the tops die back in the fall, mulch the area to help keep the ground from freezing, so you can leave the tubers until needed. Because the flesh will discolor quickly, keep the tubers whole until the last minute before you are ready to use them.

Remove all the tubers from the ground when you harvest the Jerusalem artichoke.

Rhubarb

Tender red stalks used in desserts

Botanically, rhubarb is really a perennial vegetable. It will require plenty of room in a vegetable garden; however, rhubarb is one of the most low-maintenance plants you can grow. Apart from an annual mulch of manure, you can completely ignore it. Confine it to a sunny corner of the vegetable garden, and it will reward you year after year with a crop of red stalks.

When to sow: Plant in spring or fall.

How to sow: In cold areas, grow rhubarb as a long-term perennial. It is easier to buy a plant or a division from a garden center than it is to grow rhubarb from seeds. Plant where rhubarb has plenty of space to grow large. Give it at least 3 feet (90cm) each way all to itself. In mild-winter areas, the cold spell may not be long enough to break the plant's dormancy and produce stalks.

Care: Rhubarb prefers rich, well-drained soil—too heavy or wet, and the crown may rot. If flower shoots are produced, cut them off early or they will weaken the crown. If you harvest it heavily each year, mulch it each fall with well-rotted organic matter to keep it growing strongly. This will also prevent weeds.

Applying an organic mulch to the soil will help keep rhubarb growing.

Harvesting: Don't harvest in its first year of growth, but you can take a few stalks the second year. In the third year, start harvesting the young stems as they begin to appear in spring. When a stem reaches 12–15 inches (30–38cm) high, twist it as you pull it to snap it off the crown, or cut it with a sharp knife. You can harvest for up to two months; then let the plant recover. Never remove more than one-half of the leaves at any time. To prepare rhubarb for eating, cut off the leaves; these contain high levels of oxalic acid, which is poisonous if eaten.

Recommended cultivars:
• 'Canada Red' has sweet, bright red stalks and is a good choice for cool areas.
• 'Strawberry' has greenish pink stalks.
• 'Valentine' has tender, pink-red stalks and is one of the cultivars with the best flavor.

The stalks of rhubarb are used for cooking.

SMART TIP

Forcing rhubarb
You can have rhubarb earlier in the year by forcing plants into growth. Dig up old clumps, and leave them outside in fall to expose them to a couple of frosts. Then plant them in pots, and bring them into a cool but frost-free basement or garage. Cover with black plastic to exclude light, and check them every couple of weeks. After a few weeks, the stalks should be ready for cutting. You can replant forced rhubarb crowns, but wait a year before cutting again.

Strawberry

Juicy, summertime treat

There's nothing that can be compared to a warm, fully ripe strawberry straight off the plant. Simply plant a few strawberries, and after a few years you'll have more than you know what to do with! The only downside is that they fruit over a short period, but you can overcome this by planting several cultivars to spread the harvest from early summer to fall.

When to sow: Spring or fall

How to sow: Because strawberries are vulnerable to viruses and other diseases, it is always safer to purchase guaranteed virus-free started plants from a reputable garden center or mail-order supplier. Plant in rows 18 inches (45cm) apart with 3 feet (90cm) between them. Plant them at the correct depth—the top of the crown should be just above soil level. Strawberries are susceptible to many insects and diseases, including some insects that thrive in the lawn, so it is better to grow them in soil that has not been previously covered by grass. Strawberries also make attractive container plants.

Care: Keep weeds under control by mulching with straw. During cold weather, protect the plants by covering the rows with loose straw. Because blossoms are sensitive to frost, cover the rows with a row cover. As soon as the first flowers appear, cover the beds with bird netting to stop birds, squirrels, and other animals from taking the fruit. The yield of your plants will drop in the third or fourth year, so you'll need to start new plants.

Harvesting: You need to pick strawberries on the day they ripen because overripe fruit deteriorates quickly once picked. However, under-ripe fruits can be too tart. Ideally, pick every day in peak season in the morning, when the fruit is cool and the dew has dried off.

Strawberries taste best when freshly picked.

If propagating strawberries from runners, make sure they are free from disease.

Recommended cultivars:
• 'Earliglow' is an early maturing and disease-resistant cultivar.
• 'Honeoye' is resistant to diseases and has large fruit; although it is reliable, it doesn't have the best flavor.
• 'Sparkle', a late cultivar, has good flavor and is hardy, so it is a popular choice in the North.
• 'Fort Laramie' produces large, bright red fruit; it is the most cold-tolerant cultivar, so it is a good choice for the North.
• 'Ogallala' is a hardy cultivar that will tolerate dry conditions well.
• 'Ozark Beauty' provides heavy yields of large, tasty, dark red berries; it has good disease resistance.

SMART TIP

Disease control
Unfortunately, strawberry plants suffer from a lot of diseases. Leaf spots, wilt, and powdery mildew affect the leaves, while red stele, root rot, and root knot nematodes affect the crown and roots. Viruses can cause mottled and distorted leaves. Choose a disease-resistant cultivar, and clear old strawberry plants every few years to prevent diseases from becoming a problem.

Blueberry

A native American shrub

Once established, blueberry plants yield a reasonable crop of tasty, nutritious berries every year. Maintenance is easy after the initial planting, but they are particular about where they will grow. You can amend your soil or grow them in containers to provide them with acidic soil.

When to sow: Plant in fall or spring. In most areas, early spring is the best time to plant.

How to sow: Buy potted blueberries, and plant anytime in the fall or spring, provided the ground isn't frozen. Unless you have a self-pollinating type, the flowers must be cross-pollinated to produce fruit. To guarantee a good crop, plant at least two different cultivars with a similar bloom period. Plant them close together so that insects will cross-pollinate them. Space high-bush and rabbiteye types 5–6 feet (1.5–1.8m) in rows 8 feet (2.4m) apart; space low-bush types 2 feet (60cm) in rows 3–4 feet (90–120cm) apart—they will form a low hedge.

Care: Blueberries need very acidic soil. Before you think about growing blueberries in the garden, check the soil pH: it needs to be 4.5–5.0. Because blueberries root close to the surface, ensure that they are never short of water, especially after flowering and when the berries are swelling. You'll need to keep birds from stealing the ripe fruit. Erect a framework, and hang bird netting when the first fruit start to ripen.

Harvesting: The berries are ready when they develop a bluish bloom, but taste a few before picking in earnest. Once ripe, they will keep in good condition on the plant, so you don't have to pick more than once a week.

SMART TIP

Adjusting your soil

If your soil pH is in the range of 5.0–6.0, you can still grow blueberries successfully. You'll need to add plenty of sphagnum peat or other acidic organic matter. You can also add granular sulfur to further acidify the top few inches. These plants like plenty of organic matter, such as compost, leaves, and manure. If your soil is above 6.0, consider growing blueberries in containers, or prepare a special bed for them, replacing the existing soil with something that is more suitable. Each year, add mulch and check the soil pH. If necessary, adjust the pH with granular sulfur.

Recommended types and cultivars:

• Low-Bush blueberries are the hardiest type. The plants reach 1–3 feet (30–90cm) high and spread up to 8 feet (2.4m). Good cultivars include 'Butte' and 'Top Hat'.
• High-Bush types are slightly less hardy, but they should grow in most areas. In the South and some other regions, these can make big plants up to 6 feet (1.8m) high and wide. Good cultivars include 'Bluecrop' (mid-season), 'Bluejay' (mid-season), 'Blueray' (mid), 'Chandler' (mid-late), 'Earliblue' (early), 'Herbert' (mid), 'Ivanhoe' (early), 'Jersey' (late), all good for most areas. In warm areas, choose 'O'Neal' or 'Sharpblue'.
• Half-High types are crosses between the low-bush and high-bush types, and produce bushes reaching 2–4 feet (60–120cm) high and wide with big berries. Good cultivars include 'Early Bluejay' (early), 'Northblue' (mid-season), 'Northcountry' (mid), 'Northland' (mid-season), and 'Patriot' (early).
• 'Rabbiteye' blueberries are the least hardy, but they will tolerate dry soils and are a good choice for warm regions. However, they need a winter chilling period, so they are not suitable for areas with very mild winters. They make the biggest plants, up to 15 feet (4.5m) high and 6 feet (1.8m) wide. Good cultivars include 'Bonita', 'Beckyblue', 'Climax', and 'Tifblue' (all mid-season).

Blueberries are attractive plants to keep in a container on the patio.

Blackberry

Sweet, plump, deep-colored berries

Blackberries and raspberries are both brambles, but they differ in two respects. Blackberries don't sucker—instead, each shoot roots when the tip touches the ground and produces a new plant. The berries won't let you know when they are ready to pick, either—unlike raspberries, the central plug usually comes away with the berries. Otherwise, these two berries are grown in the same way.

When to sow: Blackberries are suitable for all but the coldest and warmest zones. Buy plants in the dormant season to plant in the spring in cold areas and fall or spring in warm areas, any time the ground is not frozen.

How to sow: Follow the advice for raspberries. (See "Raspberry," page 91.) Blackberries are more vigorous than raspberries, so space them 5 feet (1.5m) apart in rows 6 feet (1.8m) apart.

Care: Prepare the soil deeply with plenty of organic matter. Remove perennial weeds. Provide support by growing blackberries against a fence. Or provide a post-and-wire trellis, and tie in the new shoots regularly.

Training a blackberry up a trellis is a way to make picking the berries easier.

The berries will turn a deep black color as they ripen.

Like raspberries, blackberries fruit on 1-year-old canes, so you won't get a crop the first year. In subsequent years, tie the new canes to a fence or trellis. Cut old canes to the ground after they have finished fruiting.

Harvesting: The fruit is ready to be picked when it reaches full size and is black and lustrous. Picking the fruit will encourage the plant to produce larger fruit later. If you are worried about insects lurking inside the fruit, soak the berries in salted water to expel them.

Recommended cultivars:
• 'Chester' is a hardy cultivar with thornless canes that produce large, firm, but not tart, berries.
• 'Ebony King' is another hardy blackberry with thornless, semi-upright canes; the plant will produce large, sweet, juicy berries.
• 'Triple Crown' has vigorous thornless canes with large juicy berries; this is a good heat-tolerant cultivar.

Currant & Gooseberry

Great berries for pies, purees, and preserves

Currants and the gooseberry both belong to the *Ribes* species, and these plants are grown in the same way. They make neat bushes, needing no support and only a little pruning each year to keep them productive. Once established, they should keep going for years. The berries are sweet when ripe, with more than a hint of acid.

When to sow: Spring or fall

How to sow: Currants and gooseberries are sold in containers or as bare-root plants in spring or fall—look for plants that are fresh out of the ground with a good ratio of root to top growth. Buy 1-year-old plants. Plant bare-root types immediately, or if the ground is not ready, bury the roots in a pot of moist potting mix to keep them from drying out. Better still, look for plants in large pots ready to put straight into the garden. Give the plants an area 4–5 feet (1.2–1.5m) in diameter each or plant 4–5 feet (1.2–1.5m) apart in rows.

Care: Both currants and gooseberries are easygoing plants. If you can, dig or till the soil deeply, and work in some compost or organic matter before planting. In subsequent years, apart from keeping the area around the plants free of weeds and providing a little general-purpose fertilizer, they require little attention. As with all fruit that grow on bushes, cover the ground around the plants with mulch, such as compost or other organic matter. It will help take care of the weeds, retain moisture, and provide sufficient nutrients. Alternatively, use a plastic sheet combined with an annual fertilizer.

Growing restrictions

The gooseberry and black currant are affected by a disease known as white pine blister rust. It hardly affects these plants, but it is a devastating disease on its alternate host, the native white pine. Thus, currants have a bad reputation. There are laws in many states on planting currants and gooseberries if there are stands of white pine nearby. Catalogs usually list restricted states because it is illegal to ship the plants to them. Check with your local Cooperative Extension Service to see what the restrictions are in your area before you plant any of these fruit.

Harvesting: The trick with all members of this family is to leave the fruit on the plant as long as possible. Pick too soon, and they will be too tart—and you'll have to add pounds of sugar to make them palatable. Let them ripen fully on the plant, and they'll become sweet. When you can eat a black currant or gooseberry straight off the bush without wincing, the berries are ready to be picked.

Recommended types and cultivars:

• Black currant types have "strigs" of fairly large, rich black fruit and are sweet when fully ripe. 'Ben Sarek' is a modern Scottish cultivar that makes a compact bush with large berries and is ideal for smaller gardens; 'Consort' is a classic blister rust-resistant cultivar.
• Red currant types bear long "strigs" of small, bright red, sharp fruit, ideal for making jelly. 'Red Lake' is popular but susceptible to powdery mildew. 'Redstart' is a high-yielding cultivar.
• White currant types are similar to red currant types, but the fruit is semitransparent, yellowish white in color, and fairly tart. 'White Imperial' is a widely grown cultivar.
• Gooseberry types have been bred with few spines. The fruit ripen to gold or red. 'Captivator' is a mildew-resistant, nearly thornless cultivar with tasty pink berries. 'Invicta', a mildew-resistant cultivar, has tart, pale green fruit good for cooking. 'Pixwell' is a variety with medium-size berries that ripen to pink. 'Poorman' has large red fruit that can be eaten fresh.
• Jostaberry is a cross that combines the larger fruit of a gooseberry with the rich color of a black currant and a taste somewhere between the two; it is resistant to blister rust and mildew.

Gooseberries (center) and currants appear different, but they are related.

Grape

Grape

Trailing vines of sweetness

There are two approaches to growing grape vines. Train them as climbers on an arbor and appreciate their shade, or train them to maximize the harvest of juicy grapes.

When to sow: Spring

How to sow: Buy strong 1-year-old plants from a garden center. Choose a type suited to your location, particularly if you live in a cool area. Plant in the spring in rows with 8 feet (2.4m) between plants. If you plant more than one row, space them 8 feet (2.4m) apart, too.

Care: Grapes prefer deep, sandy soil that warms up quickly in spring and drains quickly. It should be fertile but not too rich. Too many nutrients will encourage leaf growth, not fruit. The vines will need training along wires. Put these in place when you plant the row. In the first year, water the plants to help them become established and let them build up strong roots. Mulch around the plants to warm the soil, retain soil moisture, and suppress weeds. Train American and European grapes in early spring in the second year, before the buds break. Cut back the plant to a single stem with no sideshoots. Let four buds develop into sideshoots, two in each direction. As they grow, tie them to support wires. In the third year, fruit will grow along the sideshoots. Let four buds grow from the main stem to replace the fruiting branches the next year. In early winter, cut back the branches that bore fruit to the main stem; tie the replacement shoots to the wires, and remove all other growth. Repeat each year.

Harvesting: Leave the bunches on the vine as long as you can because grapes do not continue to ripen after being picked. When ripe they will be their full color and have a "bloom," and the bunches will detach easily from the vine.

Recommended types and cultivars:
• 'American grapes have skin that slips free from the flesh of the grape. Good cultivars include 'Canadice' and 'Reliance', which are both red-skinned and seedless; 'Concord Seedless', a seedless version of a favorite blue-skinned grape; 'Glenora', a hardy cultivar with black, seedless grapes; and 'Marquis', a white, seedless cultivar.
• European cultivars are best in warm areas; the skin on the fruit adheres to the flesh.
• Hybrids between American and European types will grow in cool areas. Good cultivars include 'Himrod Seedless' and 'Lakeland Seedless'.
• 'Muscadine grapes are native to the southern states and grow well in warm areas. They have tougher skins than other grapes that turn bronze to dark purple. Cultivars include 'Carlos' and 'Ison'.

A tepee can support grapes if an arbor, fence, or wall space is not available.

SMART TIP

Disease control
Grape vines are attacked by several diseases. Circular reddish spots with a black margin indicate black rot, while yellow spots with a downy mold on the undersides indicate downy mildew. Both diseases also attack the flowers, resulting in either shriveled or moldy fruit later. Both can be controlled by modern fungicides, but removing leaf debris in fall will help prevent the diseases from surviving over the winter.

Raspberry

Brightly colored, plump delicious berries

Once raspberries start producing fruit, it can be hard to keep up with them. Summer raspberries fruit on 1-year-old stems, referred to as "canes," which are best grown supported between parallel wires attached to posts. At the end of each summer, the canes produced in that year are tied to the wire frame to support next year's berries, while the old canes that bore fruit are cut down to the ground. Everbearing raspberries fruit on the current season's canes in midsummer and again in fall, and they don't need any permanent support. Grow both kinds, and choose an early and a late summer cultivar—and you'll have fresh raspberries until fall.

When to sow: Spring or fall

How to sow: Buy guaranteed disease-free canes from a reputable supplier in the dormant season. Raspberry canes are often sold as bare-root plants. Check that they are not dry and that they have at least one stem about ½ inch (1.3cm) or a little less in diameter and with plenty of root. When you get bare-root plants home, plant immediately if possible. If not, dig a hole and bury the roots to keep them cool and moist. Plant raspberries 2 feet (60cm) apart and rows 6 feet (1.8m) apart. Put in the supports before planting. Plant them just slightly deeper than they were originally growing. Water the canes well, and keep them moist until the plants are well established and growing strongly. Cut the original shoots back to about 2 inches (5cm) from the soil surface. Be warned: once raspberries are established, they spread and can take over the whole fruit patch!

Care: If you prepare the bed well by digging it deeply and working in plenty of compost or well-rotted manure, there will be only a little work each spring. Simply add a generous mulch of organic matter to feed the canes, retain moisture, and suppress weeds. A drip irrigation system or soaker hose is a good idea. Once the canes are established, you may need to dig out suckers that stray too far from the original row. The canes grow in the first season. In the second, they produce fruit, so you'll always have a mixture of fruiting and new canes. At the end of the season for summer berries, cut old canes down to the ground and tie in new canes.

Harvesting: Raspberries are ready to pick as soon as they reach full size and are bright red (or bright yellow in yellow-fruit cultivars, or black in black-fruit cultivars). Ripe fruit should fall off the plant easily when touched, leaving the green plug attached to the cane. Be careful when handling ripe fruit because raspberries are easily damaged; use shallow containers to avoid piling them too deeply, which can crush them. They are best eaten freshly picked but can be refrigerated for a few days.

Recommended cultivars:

- 'Bristol' is a summer-fruiting cultivar that produces vigorous upright canes with large, dark berries.
- 'Caroline' is a newer everbearing cultivar with tasty fruit.
- 'Fallgold' is an unusual everbearer with golden fruit.
- 'Fall red' is an everbearing cultivar with bright red fruit.
- 'Heritage', a popular everbearing cultivar, produces sweet red berries.
- 'Jewel', a summer-fruiting cultivar, has vigorous upright canes and is early ripening; it is disease resistant and winter hardy.
- 'Kilarney', a midseason summer-fruiting cultivar, has sweet, bright red berries; it is hardy.
- 'Latham' is an easy-to-pick, midseason summer-fruiting cultivar.
- 'Royalty' produces large, sweet purple berries on vigorous summer-fruiting canes.
- 'Tulameen', a late summer-fruiting cultivar, has heavy yields of tasty, dark pink fruit; very hardy.

There's nothing like the first ripe raspberries of the summer.

glossary

Acid soil A soil that tests lower than 7.0 on the pH scale.

Alkaline soil A soil that tests higher than 7.0 on the pH scale.

Amendments Organic or inorganic materials that improve soil structure, drainage, and nutrient-holding capacity. Some add nutrients.

Annual A plant that completes its entire life cycle in one growing season.

***Bacillus thuringiensis* (Bt)** A naturally occurring bacteria that is lethal to caterpillars but harmless to other animals. It is sold as a soluble powder to kill caterpillar pests.

Balanced fertilizer A fertilizer with equal parts of the three main nutrients needed by plants: nitrogen, phosphorous, and potassium.

Bare-root Plants that have been grown in the soil, then lifted out of it and sold to gardeners without being planted in pots.

Beneficial nematodes Minute worms that can be bought and spread on the ground to kill soil pests.

Biennial A plant that produces a storage root in its first year and flowers in the second year; most root crops are biennials.

Blanch To cover plants to exclude light, which makes the leaves or hearts pale and mild in taste.

Bolting When a plant sends up a flower stalk early due to unfavorable growing conditions. See also *Interruption of growth*.

Bordeaux mixture A mixture of simple chemicals originally used to control diseases on vines but useful on other fruit, too. However, the mixture does not wash away from foliage easily and can eventually build to toxic levels.

Brassica The family of plants that includes cabbage and its many edible relatives, from turnips to cauliflowers.

Broadcast To scatter seeds in patches, rather than along single rows, to produce a mass of leaves, a technique often useful for growing salad greens.

Canker A dead spot on a plant stem resulting from a disease caused by a fungus or bacterium.

Cloche See *Hot cap*.

Cold frame An outdoor, boxlike structure with a plastic or glass top similar to a window that is used for starting seeds and protecting young plants in cold weather.

Compost Dead plant matter collected into a pile that decomposes; it produces material that can be used as a mulch, a soil additive, or an amendment.

Cover crop A crop grown not to eat but to cover bare soil to keep it in good shape. See *Green manure*.

Crop rotation A method of preventing pests and diseases by moving plants to a different part of the vegetable garden each year in a particular sequence.

Cultivar Short for "cultivated variety." Rather than occurring naturally in the wild, cultivars are developed. Cultivar names are enclosed in single quotation marks. See *Variety*.

Cut-and-come-again A technique of cutting salad greens so that the plants resprout to provide a second and third crop of leaves.

Determinate Plants, such as tomatoes, that produce most of their fruit at the same time. See *Indeterminate*.

Dibble A tool with a pointed end that increases in diameter, used for making planting holes in the soil.

Division A propagation method that separates a plant into two or more pieces, each with at least some healthy leaves and some roots.

Dormant The state of a plant when it is alive but not actively growing. Plants may be dormant when conditions are not suitable—for example, during winter when the temperature is cold.

Draw hoe A hoe with the blade at right angles to the handle, which is pulled toward you to remove weeds.

F1 hybrid Seeds produced by crossing two specific parent types. See *Hybrid*.

Fertilizer Any product containing a concentrated form of nutrients that plants need to grow. Fertilizers can contain man-made chemicals or products of natural origin—the latter is an organic fertilizer.

Floating row cover A translucent material made from spun plastic used to cover crops, keeping them warm while letting in air and rain; it also keeps out insect pests.

Foliar feeding To spray a plant's leaves with a fertilizer containing immediately available nutrients.

Forcing To cover crops before they begin their normal growth to produce pale tender leaves or hearts.

Full sun A site that receives six or more hours a day of direct sunlight.

Fungicide A chemical or natural product used to kill or prevent diseases caused by fungi.

Furrow A narrow, shallow trench made in the soil so that seeds are buried at the correct depth and in straight lines.

Green manure A cover crop grown especially to dig into the soil to add organic matter. After green manuring soils are easier to work. See *Cover crop*.

Handpick To rid insects or other small garden pests from plants by removing them by hand.

Hand pull Removing weed seedlings by hand from among rows of crops, where a hoe cannot be used.

Harden off To acclimatize plants that have been started indoors to outdoor conditions.

Hardiness/hardy A plant's ability to survive the climate in an area without protection from winter cold or summer heat, often described in relation to official Hardiness Zones.

Hardpan A layer of hard soil beneath the surface often caused by repeatedly cultivating to the same depth. It can lead to poor drainage and poor root growth.

Heirloom An open-pollinated plant that has been around for a long time (usually from before 1940) that is sometimes kept going by gardening enthusiasts.

Herbicide A chemical for killing weeds.

Hilling A technique by which seeds are planted in a small hill, or mound, of soil, usually about 12 inches (30cm) high. This hill protects the neck of the plants, which are susceptible to rotting.

Horticultural oil A solution of natural oils used to kill insect pests, acceptable to organic gardeners.

Hot cap A temporary transparent cover for individual plants to protect them from cold weather. See *Cloche*.

Hybrid A plant resulting from crossbreeding parent plants that belong to different cultivars, species, or sometimes, genera. See *F1 Hybrid*.

Indeterminate Plants, especially tomatoes, that continue to produce fruit through the summer. See *Determinate*.

Insecticidal soap A natural product used to kill insects, acceptable to organic gardeners.

Insecticide A chemical to kill insects. Most are developed from man-made chemicals, but some are produced from naturally occurring chemicals, suitable for organic gardening.

Interruption of growth A setback to a plant due to drought, cold, or heat that stops it from growing or makes it flower early. See *Bolting*.

Invasive A plant that spreads easily and thus invades adjacent areas.

Leaf mold A compost made from leaves collected in fall; they rot slowly, so they are often kept separate from other garden waste in the compost pile.

Legume A family of plants that includes peas and beans; all have the ability to turn nitrogen in the air into nitrogen salts they can use as food.

Loam A soil that contains a fertile mixture of sand, clay, and silt.

Microclimate Conditions of sun, shade, exposure, wind, drainage, and other factors at a particular site that differ from the surrounding area. These sites can be small—sometimes only a few square feet, such as a section of a vegetable garden near a brick or stone wall that can have climate conditions that differ from those of a nearby open flower bed.

Milky spore disease A solution of a natural bacteria that kills the grubs of Japanese beetles.

Mulch A layer of material laid over the surface of the soil to retain moisture, prevent weeds from growing, or protect it from cold, heat, and wind. It may be organic, such as compost, or inorganic, such as a plastic sheet.

Nematodes Minute worms that are abundant in the soil. Although they are mostly harmless, there are a few that can damage garden plants.

NPK The ratio of the main plant nutrients in a fertilizer—nitrogen, phosphorus, and potassium are specified on the package in percentages, such as 7:7:7.

Open-pollinated Seeds collected from plants that have been pollinated naturally; the seeds produce plants that will be slightly different from their parents.

Organic Anything that is of plant or animal origin; also used to describe a way of gardening that uses only natural materials.

Organic matter Bulky material, such as manure or garden compost, that is used to improve soil and feed plants.

Overwinter The term for keeping plants growing through the winter in order to provide a crop the following spring; also refers to when insects and other creatures can survive outdoors during the winter.

Perennial A plant that normally lives for three or more years.

Pest Any insect or animal that is detrimental to the health of a plant.

Pesticide A substance that kills insect pests. The term is also used to describe other agricultural toxins, including fungicides and herbicides.

pH Literally, potential of hydrogen. A measure of acidity or alkalinity. The pH scale runs from 0 to 14, with 7 representing neutral. A pH higher than 7 is alkaline; a pH less than 7 is acidic.

Plug A small but well-rooted seedling raised in a cellular tray.

Propagate Methods, such as taking cuttings, used to create more plants. Plants also reproduce, or propagate, themselves.

Pruning The cutting and trimming of plants to remove dead wood.

Push hoe A hoe with a flat blade that extends from the end of the handle. It is pushed away from you to remove weeds.

Repot To move a seedling or a started plant into a larger pot.

Root nodule Lumps on the roots of peas and beans that convert nitrogen in the air into food.

Runner A low-growing stem that arises from the crown and runs along the ground. Runners can root at every node.

Scoville Scale Measures the amount of heat as defined by the levels of capsaicin found in chili peppers.

Seed-starter tray A plastic tray divided into square divisions; a seed sown in each will produce an easily separated seedling to plant.

Set Onion bulbs that are ready to grow into plants; they are an alternative to seeds.

Side-dress To scatter fertilizer along a row of half-grown vegetables to boost its yield.

Slow release A fertilizer that is made to release its nutrients over a period of weeks or months instead of all at once.

Species A group of plants that shares many characteristics and can interbreed freely.

Successional sowing Sowing small amounts of seeds of a particular vegetable several times during the season instead of just sowing once. This helps to spread out the harvesting period.

Tender A plant that does not survive cold conditions or frosts.

Thinning The act of removing extra seedlings from a row to provide sufficient growing space for the remaining plants.

Tilth The condition of the soil after it has been broken down and raked to create a fine, crumbly texture suitable for planting seeds.

Top-dress Scattering fertilizer over the soil before sowing a crop; it does not need to be mixed in.

Transplant A young plant grown from a seed in a pot to be planted outside when conditions are suitable; also the act of planting out started plants.

Tuber A swollen underground stem; both roots and shoots grow from tubers.

Variegated Foliage that is marked, striped, or blotched with a color other than the basic green of the leaf.

Variety See *Cultivar*.

index

Note:The numbers in **bold** indicate the main section on the subject.